This Book Is a Complete Study Guide to the Online Course.

The course is free to all InterNACHI members.

Upon successfully completing the online course and passing the final exam, you will receive a Certificate of Completion and be able to:

- perform a mold inspection;
- describe different types of mold;
- explain health effects;
- perform sampling;

- interpret lab reports
- recognize remediation efforts; and
- convey methods to help prevent mold growth.

Take the online course at **www.nachi.org/moldcourse**

How to Perform Mold Inspections

A mold inspection is a specialized type of inspection that goes beyond the scope of a general home inspection. The purpose of this publication is to provide accurate and useful information for performing mold inspections of residential buildings. This book covers the science, properties and causes of mold, as well as the potential hazards it presents to structures and to occupants' health. Inspectors will learn how to inspect and test for mold both before and after remediation. This textbook is designed to augment the student's knowledge in preparation for InterNACHI's online Mold Inspection Course and Exam (www.nachi.org). This manual also provides a practical reference guide for use on site at inspections.

To order additional training books, visit www.InspectorOutlet.com

Authors:

Ben Gromicko, Director of Education, International Association of Certified Home Inspectors; Nick Gromicko, Founder, International Association of Certified Home Inspectors, and Founder, International Association of Certified Indoor Air Consultants

Contributors:

Ron Cleland, Roy Lewis, Manny Marinos, Michael Marlow, Randy Mayo, Erik Schmidt & Nate Snook

Graphics:

Levi Nelson, Jackson Tupper, Erica Saurey & Chris Krowiak

Editor:

Kate Tarasenko / Crimea River

Layout & Design:

Jessica Langer

www.NACHI.org

Table of Contents

Overview

Overall Objectives

The purpose of this manual is to define and teach the industry's best practices for conducting a mold inspection of a building. The student will learn how to find and report mold growth that may exist in a building using a visual examination and mold sampling of the building.

The student will learn:

- what mold is;
- the Mold Inspection Standards of Practice of IAC2, the International Association of Certified Indoor Air Consultants;
- the potential health effects related to mold exposure;
- what mold needs to grow;
- how to perform a visual examination of a building to find mold;
- how to utilize the IAC2 Mold Sampling Decision Chart;
- the proper use of tools;
- the appropriate equipment and PPE;
- hypotheses development;
- building science and moisture;
- sampling devices and procedures;
- documentation of work;
- how to interpret laboratory results;
- mold remediation;
- report writing; and
- how to prevent mold growth.

This manual is designed primarily for residential home inspection professionals. Public health and environmental health professionals who are involved with mold issues may also be interested in this book. Building managers, custodians, remediators, contractors, and other professionals who respond to mold problems may also want to refer to this textbook.

Learning Objectives

The student-professional will demonstrate an understanding and comprehension of this manual by reading and studying the material, taking the practice quizzes at the end of selected sections, and by taking the online course in its entirety (identical to this book), and successfully passing a timed online exam.

Note:

The U.S. Environmental Protection Agency (EPA) does not define safety limits for mold or mold spores in the air. There are no federal or state threshold limit values for inspectors to use when interpreting results of mold spores in an indoor environment. There are no federal or state requirements for inspectors in the sampling of mold. Research of the most accepted, best practices in the industry have been compiled here in an effort to develop a manual for mold inspection training.

Please note that the mold inspection online course and the materials on which it is based provide simple guidelines; some professionals may prefer other inspection and sampling methods. Neither the online course nor this textbook covers all situations; they do not reference all research and information sources, and they do not review all potentially useful methods, procedures or protocols. The absence of a method, standard or technique from this manual does not indicate or imply that it is not effective or important.

Research on mold and on its health effects continues. This textbook does not describe all of the potential health effects related to mold exposure; it provides only an overview. For more detailed information, consult a health professional or your state or local health department.

For a listing of sources consulted in the development of this guide, please see Section 30: Sources and Resources.

Section 1: Types of Mold Inspections

This guide categorizes two types of mold inspections. One type is the Complete Mold Inspection. The other type is the Limited Mold Inspection. All sampling is performed according to the IAC2 Mold Sampling Procedures. (Refer to Section 28: Vital Documents.)

Complete Mold Inspection

The Complete Mold Inspection is performed by an IAC2-certified mold inspector. (Refer to Section 2 of the IAC2 Mold Inspection Standards of Practice.)

The Complete Mold Inspection is performed in accordance with the Mold Inspection Standards of Practice of the International Association of Certified Indoor Air Consultants (**www.IAC2.org**).

The inspector shall perform:

- a non-invasive, visual examination of the readily accessible, visible, and installed systems and components of the building, as outlined in the IAC2 Mold Inspection Standards of Practice;

- moisture, temperature and humidity measurements;

- at least three air samples (one indoor and two outdoor); and

- possibly one surface sampling at an area of concern.

The inspector shall report:

- moisture intrusion;

- water damage;

- musty odors;

- apparent mold growth;

- conditions conducive to mold growth;

- the results of a laboratory analysis of all mold samplings taken at the building; and

- any system or components listed in the Standards of Practice that were not visually examined, and the reasons they were not inspected.

Unless the inspector and client agree to a limitation of the inspection, the inspection will be performed on the primary building and attached parking structure.

A Complete Mold Inspection includes:

- a visual examination of the entire building, its systems and components;

- moisture, temperature and humidity measurements; and

- taking mold samples.

Limited Mold Inspection

The Limited Mold Inspection is performed by an IAC2-certified mold inspector. (Refer to Section 3 of the IAC2 Mold Inspection Standards of Practice.)

The difference between a Complete Mold Inspection and a Limited Mold Inspection is a limitation of the non-invasive, visual examination of the building. The Limited Mold Inspection does not include a visual examination of the entire building, but is limited to a specific area of the building identified and defined by the inspector.

Prior to the inspection, the inspector and client shall agree to the limitations of the visual examination. As a result, potential sources of mold growth in other areas of the building may not be inspected.

The inspector shall perform:

- a non-invasive, visual examination of the readily accessible, visible, and installed systems and components of only the specific room or area defined by the inspector;
- at least three air samples (one indoor and two outdoor); and
- possibly one surface sampling at an area of concern.

The inspector shall report:

- moisture intrusion;
- water damage;
- musty odors;
- apparent mold growth;
- conditions conducive to mold growth; and
- the results of a laboratory analysis of all mold samplings taken at the building.

The Limited Mold Inspection is a fast and affordable way to confirm the existence of mold and, if possible, determine the type of mold present in a specific, defined area of the building.

An example of a Limited Mold Inspection:

The inspector's client requests a Limited Mold Inspection to be performed. The scope is specifically limited to the under-floor crawlspace of the building. Only the crawlspace will be inspected, including a non-invasive examination of the crawlspace. At least one mold sample will be taken, typically a tape sample, if apparent mold is visible.

A Limited Mold Inspection includes:

- visual examination limited to a specific, defined area of the building; and
- mold samples.

Quiz on Section 1

1. T/F: The attached parking structure is not within the scope of a complete mold inspection.

    ☐ True
    ☐ False

2. T/F: The inspector shall report musty odors.

    ☐ True
    ☐ False

3. There are two types of mold inspections taught in this guide. One is a Limited Mold Inspection. The other is a _____ Mold Inspection.

    ☐ Clearance
    ☐ Complete
    ☐ Incomplete
    ☐ Partial
    ☐ Screen

4. T/F: The visual examination of a building is non-invasive.

    ☐ True
    ☐ False

5. T/F: At least one air sample is required as part of a Complete Mold Inspection.

    ☐ True
    ☐ False

6. T/F: All sampling shall be performed according to the IAC2 Mold Sampling Procedures available at **www.IAC2.org**.

    ☐ True
    ☐ False

Answer Key is on page 148.

Section 2: IAC2 Mold Inspection Standards

In the previous section, we learned about the two types of mold inspections. A mold inspection requires the inspector to perform them according to a standard. The following are the IAC2 Mold Inspection Standards of Practice.

An updated version of the IAC2 Mold Inspection Standards of Practice can be found online at **www.iac2.org/sop.php**. These standards are subject to change as more credible information about fungal contaminants becomes available. The standards may be updated at any time. It is the inspector's responsibility to know the standards and apply them.

Table of Contents

2.1 Scope

The purpose of this standard is to provide standardized procedures to be used for a mold inspection. There are two types of mold inspections described in the IAC2 Mold Inspection Standards of Practice:

1) the Complete Mold Inspection (see Section 2.2); and

2) the Limited Mold Inspection (see Section 2.3).

    2.1.1 Unless the inspector and client agree to a limitation of the inspection, the inspection will be performed at the primary building and attached parking structure. Detached structures shall be inspected separately.

    2.1.2 A mold inspection is valid for the date of the inspection and cannot predict future mold growth. Because conditions conducive to mold growth in a building can vary greatly over time, the results of a mold inspection (examination and sampling) can be relied upon only for the point in time at which the inspection was conducted.

    2.1.3 A mold inspection is not a home (property) inspection.

    2.1.4 A mold inspection is not a comprehensive indoor air-quality inspection.

    2.1.5 A mold inspection is not intended to eliminate the uncertainty or the risk of the presence of mold, or the adverse effects mold may cause to a building or its occupants.

2.2 Complete Mold Inspection

I. The inspector shall perform:

- a non-invasive, visual examination of the readily accessible, visible, and installed systems and components of the building (listed in Section 2.4: Standards of Practice);

- moisture, temperature and humidity measurements (refer to Section 2.4.8: Moisture, Humidity and Temperature); and

- mold samples according to the IAC2 Mold Sampling Procedures (refer to Section 2.5: IAC2 Mold Sampling Procedures).

II. The inspector shall report:

- moisture intrusion;

- water damage;

- musty odors;

- apparent mold growth;

- conditions conducive to mold growth;

- the results of a laboratory analysis of all mold samples taken at the building; and

- any system or components listed in Section 2.4: Standards of Practice that were not inspected, and the reasons they were not inspected.

2.3 Limited Mold Inspection

The Limited Mold Inspection does not include a visual examination of the entire building, but is limited to a specific area of the building identified and described by the inspector. As a result, moisture intrusion, water damage, musty odors, apparent mold growth, and/or conditions conducive to mold growth in other areas of the building may not be inspected.

I. The inspector shall describe:

- the room or limited area of the building in which the Limited Mold Inspection is performed.

II. The inspector shall perform:

- a limited, non-invasive, visual examination of the readily accessible, visible, and installed systems and components located only in the room or limited area (as described in the previous section); and
- mold samples according to the IAC2 Mold Sampling Procedures (see Section 2.5 IAC2: Mold Sampling Procedures).

III. The inspector shall report:

- moisture intrusion;
- water damage;
- musty odors;
- apparent mold growth;
- conditions conducive to mold growth; and
- the results of a laboratory analysis of all mold samples taken at the building.

2.4 Standards of Practice

2.4.1 Roof

I. The inspector shall inspect from the ground level or eaves:

A. the roof covering;

B. the roof drainage system, including gutters and downspouts; and

C. the vents, flashings, skylights, chimneys, and any other roof penetrations.

II. The inspector is not required to:

A. walk on any roof surface;

B. predict the service-life expectancy; or

C. perform a water test.

2.4.2 Exterior and Grounds

I. The inspector shall inspect from the ground level:

   A. the cladding, flashing and trim;

   B. exterior doors, windows, decks, stoops, steps, stairs, porches, railings, eaves, soffits and fascias;

   C. the exterior grading surrounding the building's perimeter; and

   D. items that penetrate the exterior siding or covering materials.

II. The inspector is not required to:

   A. inspect underground drainage systems;

   B. inspect window-well drainage; or

   C. inspect defects not related to mold growth or moisture intrusion.

2.4.3 Basement, Foundation, Crawlspace and Structure

I. The inspector shall inspect:

   A. the foundation, basement and/or crawlspace, including ventilation; and

   B. for moisture intrusion.

II. The inspector is not required to:

   A. operate sump pumps with inaccessible floats; or

   B. inspect for structural defects not related to mold growth or moisture intrusion.

2.4.4 Heating, Cooling and Ventilation

I. The inspector shall inspect:

   A. the air handler, circulating fan and air filter;

   B. the condensate pump;

   C. readily visible ductwork;

   D. a representative number of supply and return air registers;

   E. the central humidifier; and

   F. the central air-conditioning unit.

II. The inspector is not required to:

   A. inspect the air-conditioning coil, if not readily accessible;

   B. inspect the condensate pan, if not readily accessible;

   C. test the performance or efficiency of the HVAC system; or

   D. inspect the interior of the ductwork system.

2.4.5 Plumbing

I. The inspector shall inspect:

   A. the readily visible main water line;

   B. the readily visible water supply lines;

   C. the readily visible drain, waste and vent pipes;

   D. the hot water source; and

   E. fixtures such as toilets, faucets, showers and tubs.

II. The inspector is not required to:

   A. test the showers or tubs by filling them with water;

   B. test whirlpool tubs, saunas, steam rooms or hot tubs; or

   C. inspect for plumbing defects that are not related to mold growth or moisture intrusion.

2.4.6 Attic, Ventilation and Insulation

I. The inspector shall inspect:

   A. the insulation;

   B. ventilation of attic spaces; and

   C. framing and sheathing.

II. The inspector is not required to:

   A. move, touch or disturb insulation;

   B. inspect for vapor retarders; or

   C. break or otherwise damage the surface finish or weather seal on or around access panels and covers.

2.4.7 Interior

I. The inspector shall inspect:

   A. the walls, ceilings, floors, doors and windows;

   B. the ventilation in the kitchen, bathrooms and laundry room; and

   C. whole-house ventilation fans.

II. The inspector is not required to:

   A. inspect for interior defects that are not related to mold growth or moisture intrusion.

2.4.8 Moisture, Humidity and Temperature

I. The inspector shall measure:

A. moisture of any room or area of the building that has moisture intrusion, water damage, moldy odors, apparent mold growth, or conditions conducive to mold growth;

B. the humidity of any room or area of the building (at the inspector's discretion); and

C. the temperature of any room or area of the building (at the inspector's discretion).

2.5 IAC2 Mold Sampling Procedures

Table of Contents

2.5.1 General Comments

• Use the IAC2 Mold Sampling Decision Chart and the IAC2 Standards of Practice to assist in deciding when and where to take samples in a building.

• Samples of the indoor air and the outside air should be taken for comparison. There should not be any mold inside the house that is not found outside. The concentration of mold inside a home should not be higher than the concentration of mold outside.

- Keep in mind that mold spores in the air being sampled can vary greatly in relation to the life cycle of the mold, atmospheric and environmental conditions, and the amount of ventilation. There is seasonal and diurnal variability in airborne mold at an indoor, residential environment.

- Air sampling may be necessary if the presence of mold is suspected (if, for example, musty odors are noted) but cannot be identified by a visual examination. The purpose of such air sampling is to determine the location and/or extent of mold contamination. All mold spores have a source, and identifying the source is the goal.

- Because the outdoor sample is the control sample and is used to compare with the indoor sample, the samples should be collected as close as possible in time and under similar conditions. Air samples should be collected at the same air-flow rate, for the same duration of time, near the same height above the floor in all rooms that are sampled indoors, and using the same type of collection device.

2.5.2 Air-Flow Rate

- There are many different types of air pumps, measurement meters and spore collectors that can be used for an air sample at a mold inspection. The air pump should be adjusted to collect air at a flow rate that is recommended by the manufacturer of the collection device. The result of an air-pump sample is recorded in spores per meter, cubed (spores/m^3).

- If the air-flow rate is too fast, the spores will bounce off the collector plate or slide and will not stick. If the air-flow rate is too slow, the spores float around the collector plate or slide and will not stick.

2.5.3 Rotameter

- Rotameters are air-flow meters that provide field accuracy in an easy-to-read instrument. The principle of operation is simple: air flow passes through a vertical, tapered tube and pushes a small ball or float, having a diameter slightly less than the smaller end of the tube. As the little ball rises, the clearance between the ball and the tube wall increases. The ball becomes stationary when the diameter of the tube is large enough to allow the total air flow past the ball. The flow rate is determined by the number on the tube at the middle position of the stabilized ball.

2.5.4 Surface Sampling

- Surface sampling can provide information regarding whether the visible, apparent mold is, in fact, actual microbial growth (mold) or not, can measure the relative degree of the mold contamination, and can serve to confirm that the sampled mold growth may be producing mold spores in the air.

2.5.4.1 Area of Concern: Take One Sample

- If there is an area of concern (such as a room or area with moisture intrusion, water damage, musty odors, apparent mold growth, or conditions conducive to mold growth), the inspector shall take at least one surface sample in each area of concern.

- Additional surface samples may be taken at the discretion of the inspector.

2.5.4.2 No Areas of Concern: Not Required

- If there are no areas of concern (no moisture intrusion, no water damage, no musty odors, no apparent mold growth, and no conditions conducive to mold growth), the inspector is not required to perform a surface sampling.
- Surface samples may be taken in other areas of the building at the discretion of the inspector.

2.5.4.3 Swab

- A swab comes inside a plastic tube container. The cellulose swab is moistened with a liquid preservative stored in an ampoule at one end of the tube container. Any bacteria collected with the swab are transferred via the swab into a tube. The tube is sent directly to a laboratory for analysis.
- A swab provides immediate determination of the presence of fungal spores, as well as the types of fungi present.

2.5.4.3.1 Areas of Concern

- The inspector shall take at least one swab sample when a visual examination of the building yields moisture intrusion, water damage, apparent mold growth, musty odors, or conditions conducive to mold growth. Additional sampling may be performed at the discretion of the inspector.

2.5.4.3.2 Sampling

- Hold the tube container so that the ampoule with the liquid preservative is at the top. Pinch the plastic tube so the liquid will flow down onto the swab. To remove the moistened swab, pull on the cap. Rub and roll the wet swab over a 1-inch-square area of the apparent mold growth. The swab should collect visible apparent mold. Insert the swab back into the tube. Secure the cap.

2.5.4.3.3 Each Sample

- A unique sample number should be recorded for each swab sample. Write the number on the tube itself. The chain-of-custody document should have the sample number, location, date and time of the sampling.

2.5.4.3.4 Each Room

- Take a sample in each room or area where there is visible, apparent mold.

2.5.4.3.5 Each Color

- If there is apparent mold growth of different colors in the room or area, take a sample of each different-colored mold. The different colors may indicate different types of mold.

2.5.4.3.6 Each Substrate

- If mold is visible on different substrates or building materials, such as wood, drywall or wallpaper, then a sample from each different material is recommended.

2.5.4.4 Tape

- A tape system provides a quick way to sample visible mold. A tape-lift system is the most common surface-sampling technique. It can be used instead of a swab sampling. Many tape samples can be collected in a short period of time. Samples that show hyphae fragments and reproductive structures can provide proof of mold growth.

- There are many advantages of using tape-lift systems instead of regular tape. One of the most popular tape sampling products is Bio-Tape™. The Bio-Tape™ system is easier to handle, the tapes are individually numbered, it requires less laboratory preparation time, and the slides are flexible and will not break.

- The sampling result is not quantitative. The presence of fungi can be confirmed, genera can be identified, and possibly a semi-quantitative estimation of the amount of each genus can be determined.

2.5.4.4.1 Sampling

The steps for using a tape-lift system are as follows:

- remove the slide from the mailer;

- record the sample number and all other identification information prior to taking the sample;

- peel off the protective liner from the slide to expose the adhesive;

- place the slide with the sticky side down onto the contaminated area being sampled;

- press down gently and make contact (excessive pressure is not necessary);

- lift the slide from the surface and place it back into the slide mailer. Do not replace the protective liner;

- record all information on the chain-of-custody document, including property address, date, time and sample number; and

- mail the sample to the laboratory.

2.5.4.4.2 PPE

- Because there is direct contact with and disturbance of the contaminated area, personal protective equipment (PPE) is recommended, including gloves and a respirator rated at N-95 or higher.

2.5.4.4.3 Each Sample

- A unique sample number should be recorded for each tape sample. The chain-of-custody document should have the sample number, location, date and time of the tape sampling.

2.5.4.4.4 Each Room

- Take a tape sampling in each room or area where there is visible, apparent mold.

2.5.4.4.5 Each Color

- If there is apparent mold growth of different colors in the room or area, take a tape sample of each different-colored mold. The different colors may indicate different types of mold.

2.5.4.4.6 Each Substrate

- If mold is visible on different substrates or building materials, such as wood, drywall or wallpaper, then a tape sample from each different material is recommended.

2.5.4.5 Carpet

- A carpet tends to contain the history of any mold that has been growing in the building. The carpet sampling is performed to reveal previous mold problems. A carpet sampling can also reveal undetected mold growth that may have been covered over or cleaned up. Choose an area that is not heavily walked upon—an area with little foot traffic. Do not sample under furniture.

- A household vacuum cleaner and a carpet-sampling cartridge are used to vacuum a small area of the carpet. The cartridge should be inserted as deep into the pile of the carpet as possible. If the carpet has not been cleaned thoroughly prior to a sampling, it can easily hold evidence of a mold problem in the house. Even after cleaning, there can be mold spores discovered deep in the carpet.

2.5.4.5.1 Set-Up

- Insert the nylon filter into the collector nozzle. It should snap into place. Attach the device to the vacuum hose securely. An adapter may be needed. If the attachment is loose, use duct tape to make a tight connection.

2.5.4.5.2 Sampling

- Choose a 6-foot by 3-foot sampling area in front of a sofa or large chair where occupants spend a lot of time. Vacuum this area thoroughly. Next, select a 6-foot by 3-foot area in a bedroom alongside a bed. Remove the filter and place it into the bag that came with the unit. Mail it to the laboratory.

2.5.5 Outdoor Air Sampling

2.5.5.1 Two Outdoor Samples

- The inspector shall take two outdoor samples of the highest-quality general air to be used as control samples (or background samples). These samples are to be used for comparison with the indoor sample(s).

2.5.5.2 Upon Arrival

- The outdoor sampling should begin soon after arriving at the property, assuming that the weather is clear and calm. It is better to perform the outdoor sampling while the weather is favorable than to wait. The outdoor conditions may change drastically during the examination and sampling of the building's interior.

2.5.5.3 Weather

- Air sampling should not be conducted during unusually severe storms or periods of unusually high winds. Severe weather will affect the sampling and analysis results in several ways.

- First, a high wind will increase the variability of airborne mold-spore concentration because of wind-induced differences in air pressure between the building's interior and exterior. Second, rapid changes in barometric pressure increase the chance of a large difference in the interior and exterior air pressures, consequently changing the rate of airborne mold spores being sucked into the building. Weather predictions available on local news stations can provide sufficient information to determine if these conditions are likely.

2.5.5.3.1 Clear and Calm

- On a chain-of-custody form, the weather conditions shall be recorded. The weather conditions should be clear and calm. High winds may affect the quality of the sampling, including the comparison between indoor and outdoor samplings.

2.5.5.3.2 No Rain

- An air-pump sampling should not take place outdoors if it is raining. If possible, wait at least two hours after the rain has stopped before taking an air-pump sample. Alterations or adjustments to the normal procedure or locations of taking air-pump samples, particularly for the control sample, must be recorded in a chain-of-custody form.

2.5.5.3.3 Above Freezing

- An air-pump sampling should not take place when the outdoor air temperature is below 32° F. All air sampling should take place when the air temperature is above freezing.

2.5.5.3.4 No Snow Covering

- If the ground is completely covered with snow, outdoor air-pump sampling should not be performed. A partial covering or a light dusting of snow is acceptable.

2.5.5.3.5 Ten Minutes

- On a clear, windless day, air-pump sampling should run for 10 minutes. (Be sure to refer to the manufacturer's recommendation.) When the outdoor air is not clear and windless, then the time of the sampling should be reduced to five minutes or less. A breeze, the mowing of grass, nearby construction, and dusty air can all affect the sampling conditions.

2.5.5.4 Location

- If possible, one outdoor sample should be located on the windward side of the building (the side facing the point from which the wind blows), and the other should be located on the leeward-side of the building (the side sheltered from the wind).

- The sampling device located on the windward side of the building should be positioned so as to face the wind directly. The sampling device should point toward the wind, in the direction of the point from which the wind is blowing. The sampling device should be 3 to 6 feet from the ground surface (breathable space).

- Typically, the device should be about 10 feet away from the front entry door. The idea is to have both outdoor samples located in areas where the devices will collect a representative sampling of the air that may enter the building through the entry door or nearby open windows (the openings on the sides of the building).

2.5.5.4.1 Ten Feet

- If there is a main ventilation component of the building that draws fresh air into the building from the outdoors, the sampling should be performed 10 feet from that intake.

- The sampling should be performed at least 10 feet from the most frequently used entrance to the home.

- The air sampling devices should be kept at least 10 feet away from all openings, air intakes, registers, exhaust vents, vent pipes, ventilation fans, etc.

2.5.5.4.2 Nothing Overhead

- Sampling should not be performed under an overhang, soffit or eave, or carport, porch roof, or any other roof or overhead structure.

2.5.6 Indoor Air Sampling

2.5.6.1 Closed-Building Conditions

- Indoor air sampling should be made under closed-building conditions. Closed-building conditions are necessary in order to stabilize the air that may contain mold spores or mVOCs, and to increase the reproducibility of the air sampling and measurement.

  (Microbial volatile organic compounds, or mVOCs, are small molecules that don't tend to settle out on carpet and other surfaces the way mold spores do. They are quickly released into the air and can pass through walls, allowing them to quickly spread throughout the inside of a building. They also tend to emit a strong odor or musty smell, which is direct evidence of active or recently active mold growth.)

- Windows on all levels, as well as external doors, should be kept closed (except during normal entry and exit) during the sampling period. Normal entry and exit include a brief opening and closing of a door, but—to the extent possible—external doors should not be left open for more than a few minutes.

- In addition, external-internal air-exchange systems (other than a furnace), such as high-volume, whole-house and window fans, should not be operating. However, attic fans intended to control attic (and not whole-building) temperature and humidity should continue to operate. Combustion or make-up air supplies must not be closed.

- Normal operation of permanently installed energy-recovery ventilators (also known as heat-recovery ventilators or air-to-air heat exchangers) may also continue during closed-building conditions. In houses where permanent radon mitigation systems have been installed, these systems should be functioning during the air-sampling period.

- Closed-building conditions will generally exist as normal living conditions in northern areas of the country when the average daily temperature is low enough so that windows are kept closed. Depending on the geographical area, this can be the period from late fall to early spring.

2.5.6.2 HVAC

2.5.6.2.1 Take One Air Sample

- At least one air sample shall be taken at an air-supply register of the HVAC system. It is preferred to sample prior and during the operation of the HVAC system. If only one sampling can be performed, then the sample should be taken 15 minutes after the HVAC system is turned on.

- Ideally, there would be at least three sampling devices similarly situated throughout the building, but financial or time constraints may limit the number of samples that can be taken.

2.5.6.2.2 Location

• The air sample should be taken 3 to 5 feet from an air-supply register, with the sampling device oriented so that air from the supply register directly enters the sampling device.

2.5.6.2.3 Agitation

• A gentle or vigorous mechanical agitation of the ductwork (a bump or shake) is appropriate.

2.5.6.3 Indoor Air

2.5.6.3.1 Take One Air Sample

• The inspector shall perform at least one indoor sampling. Additional samplings may be performed at the discretion of the inspector.

2.5.6.3.2 Areas of Concern

• At least one air sample shall be taken near the center of each room or area of the building in which there are areas of concern (moisture intrusion, water damage, musty odors, visible, apparent mold growth, and/or conditions conducive to mold growth).

2.5.6.3.3 No Areas of Concern

• At least one indoor air sample shall be taken in the most lived-in common room, such as the family room or living room. (The location shall be determined at the discretion of the inspector.)

2.5.6.3.4 Location

• An indoor air sampling should only take place in a livable space in the building. Sampling in areas such as closets, under-floor crawlspaces, unfinished attics, storage or utility rooms, or inside the HVAC system is prohibited.

• The indoor air sample should be taken in the middle or center of the area or room.

• The air collection device should be placed about 3 to 6 feet above the floor's surface.

2.5.6.3.5 Ten Minutes

• Inside the building, the air-pump sampling should run for 10 minutes. If there is a lot of indoor activity, then the air-pump sampling should be reduced to five minutes. If there is an active source of dust, such as construction or cleaning, then the air sampling time should be reduced to one minute. Be sure to follow the recommendations of the manufacturer of the sampling device or collector.

2.5.6.4 Sampling

• The sampling equipment must be protected, clean, and properly maintained at all times. The sampling device shall be clean and free from dirt and debris prior to starting a sampling. If re-usable collection devices are used, then they shall be handled and cleaned prior to use, in accordance with the manufacturer's recommendation. The collector may be re-useable and have sticky slides already prepared, or the collector may be a one-time-use, self-contained device.

• Slides, cassettes, and one-time-use devices should be stored in cool, dry environments. The slides must be protected from direct sunlight. Sampling devices (slides, swabs, cassettes, tapes) older than one year should not be used.

- Set the air collector at a normal breathing height, which is about 3 to 6 feet above ground level or the floor's surface. A tripod is typically used to set the collector's height.

- Calibrate the flow of the pump. Do not attach the sampling device, cassette or collector on the tubing yet. Measure the flow rate of the pump with a rotameter that has been calibrated to a standard. Make sure that the flow rate is set to the manufacturer's recommendation. For example, an Air-O-Cell® cassette flow rate is 15 liters of air per minute. The pump should be calibrated regularly (once a day). A record of calibrations should be kept in a work ledger or log book.

- After calibration, securely attach the tubing of the pump to the sampling device or collector. Turn on the pump. Start sampling. Record the start time.

- After turning on the air pump, check the air-flow rate. The flow rate should not vary. A flow change greater than 5% requires a new air sample to be taken. All air samples must have the same volume. A digital time controller on the equipment is highly recommended.

- Examine the collector. There should not be an overload on the slide. There should be a fine trace, hardly visible to the human eye, of dust and spores on the slide. A slide that has an easily visible trace on it may be unreadable. If that is the case, the environmental conditions may need improvement or a new sampling location may be needed. If a slide is heavy, a new sample should be taken.

- Remember, all air samples must have the same volume. Refer to the manufacturer's recommendations about sampling time and volume for each type of sampling device.

- Record the time that the pump stopped. Mark the sampling device with a unique sampling number. Record that information on the chain-of-custody form.

- Place slides in a protective carrying case, or close the collector if a cassette is used. A new sample must be taken if a slide is accidentally touched, smeared or contaminated because it will be unreadable.

- Calculate the volume by multiplying the liters of air pumped by the number of minutes. An example of the calculation is 20 liters of air pumped multiplied by 10 minutes equals 20 liters per minute or 200 liters (20L x 10 minutes = 200 L).

2.6 Limitations and Exclusions

2.6.1 Limitations

I. These Standards of Practice apply only to residential buildings with four or fewer dwelling units.

II. The mold inspection is not a warranty, guarantee, or insurance policy.

III. The mold inspection is not technically exhaustive.

IV. The mold inspection will not identify concealed or latent conditions or defects.

V. The mold inspection will not identify mold growth not readily visible at the time of the inspection.

VI. The scope of a mold inspection does not include future conditions or events.

VII. The scope of a mold inspection does not include hidden mold growth or future mold growth.

2.6.2 Exclusions

I. The inspector is not required to report:

    A. the condition of any system or component that is not readily accessible;

    B. the condition of any system or component that is not in the IAC2 Standards of Practice;

    C. the service-life expectancy of any system or component;

    D. the size, capacity, BTU, performance or efficiency of any component or system;

    E. compliance with codes, regulations, or installation guidelines; or

    F. the presence of evidence of rodents, animals, insects, wood-destroying insects and/or pests.

II. The inspector is not required to:

    A. determine the presence of hidden mold by physical examination or sampling;

    B. report replacement or repair cost estimates;

    C. lift carpeting or padding;

    D. inspect any other environmental issue;

    E. determine the cause or reason of any condition;

    F. perform a geotechnical, structural or geological evaluation;

    G. move any personal items or other obstructions to the inspection, such as, but not limited to: insulation, throw rugs, furniture, floor or wall coverings, ceiling tiles, window coverings, equipment, plants, ice, debris, snow, water, dirt, foliage and/or appliances;

    H. dismantle, open or uncover any system or component;

    I. enter or access any area, crawlspace or attic space which, in the opinion of the inspector, may be unsafe or may pose a risk to personal safety;

    J. do anything that, in the inspector's opinion, may be unsafe or dangerous to the inspector or others, or potentially damage property; or

    K. determine the insurability of a property.

III. The inspector is not required to operate:

    A. any system that is shut down;

    B. any system that does not function properly;

    C. any system that does not turn on with the use of normal operating controls;

    D. any shut-off water or fuel valves, or manual stop valves;

    E. any electrical disconnect or over-current protection devices; or

    F. any irrigation or sprinkler systems.

2.7 Definitions

- **accessible:** can be approached or entered by the inspector safely, without difficulty, fear or danger.

- **apparent mold:** visible growth with characteristics of mold that cannot be confirmed by the inspector without the benefit of sampling. The term "mold growth" is interchangeable in this guide with "fungal growth" and "microbial growth."

- **area of concern:** a room or area with moisture intrusion, water damage, musty odors, visible, apparent mold growth, and/or conditions conducive to mold growth.

- **complete:** comprehensive in scope or purpose.

- **component:** a permanently installed or attached fixture, element or part of a system.

- **condition:** the visible and conspicuous state of being of an object.

- **dismantle:** to open, take apart or remove any component, device or piece that would not typically be opened, taken apart or removed by an ordinary occupant.

- **due diligence:** the degree of care and caution required by the circumstances of a person.

- **dwelling unit:** a complete place to live, which includes a kitchen and a bathroom.

- **household appliances:** kitchen and laundry appliances, room air conditioners, and similar appliances.

- **inspect:** to visually look at readily accessible systems and components safely, using normal operating controls, and accessing readily accessible panels and areas in accordance, with these Standards of Practice.

- **inspector:** one who performs an inspection.

- **interior:** the area(s) of a building where people have access and which are included in the space of the building.

- **invasive:** to probe, dismantle or take apart a system or component.

- **limited:** not comprehensive in scope or purpose.

- **microbial:** describes a microscopic organism, such as mold.

- **normal operating controls:** devices such as thermostats that would be operated by ordinary occupants, and which require no specialized skill or knowledge.

- **occupants:** tenants, persons, or entities, each of whom uses a portion of the building.

- **readily accessible:** an item or component is readily accessible if, in the judgment of the inspector, it is capable of being safely observed without movement of obstacles, detachment or disengagement of connecting or securing devices, or other unsafe or difficult procedures in order to gain access.

- **report:** a written communication (possibly including digital images) of conditions observed during the inspection.

- **representative number:** at least one in a particular room or area.

- **sampling:** the collection of air, surface and/or carpet samples for analysis.

- **shut down:** turned off, unplugged, inactive, not in service, not operational, etc.

- **system:** an assembly of various components that function as a whole.

- **technically exhaustive:** a comprehensive and detailed examination beyond the scope of a mold inspection, which would involve or include, but would not be limited to: dismantling, specialized knowledge or training, special equipment, measurements, calculations, testing, research, analysis, or other means.

- **unsafe:** a condition in a readily accessible, installed system or component, which is judged to be a significant risk of personal injury during normal, day-to-day use. The risk may be due to damage, deterioration, improper installation, or a change in accepted residential construction standards.

Quiz on Section 2

1. T/F: The mold inspection is a home (property) inspection.

 □ True
 □ False

2. T/F: The inspector shall carefully inspect the electrical panelboard.

 □ True
 □ False

3. T/F: The inspector shall identify mold growth that is not readily visible.

 □ True
 □ False

4. T/F: The inspector shall report the life expectancy of the roof covering.

 □ True
 □ False

5. T/F: Inspecting for wood-destroying insects is within the scope of a complete mold inspection.

 □ True
 □ False

6. T/F: The mold inspector is not required to lift carpeting to detect apparent mold growth.

 □ True
 □ False

7. _____ is visible growth with characteristics of mold, which cannot be confirmed by the inspector without the benefit of sampling.

 □ Actual mold
 □ Apparent mold
 □ Tested mold
 □ Confirmed mold

Answer Key is on page 148.

Section 3: What Is Mold?

In the previous sections, we learned about the types of mold inspections and the IAC2 Standards. Now let's learn about mold and what it is.

Molds are organisms that are found indoors and outdoors. They are part of the natural environment and play an important role in our ecological system by breaking down and digesting organic material. Molds are neither plants nor animals. They are part of the kingdom Fungi.

Mold Is Fungi

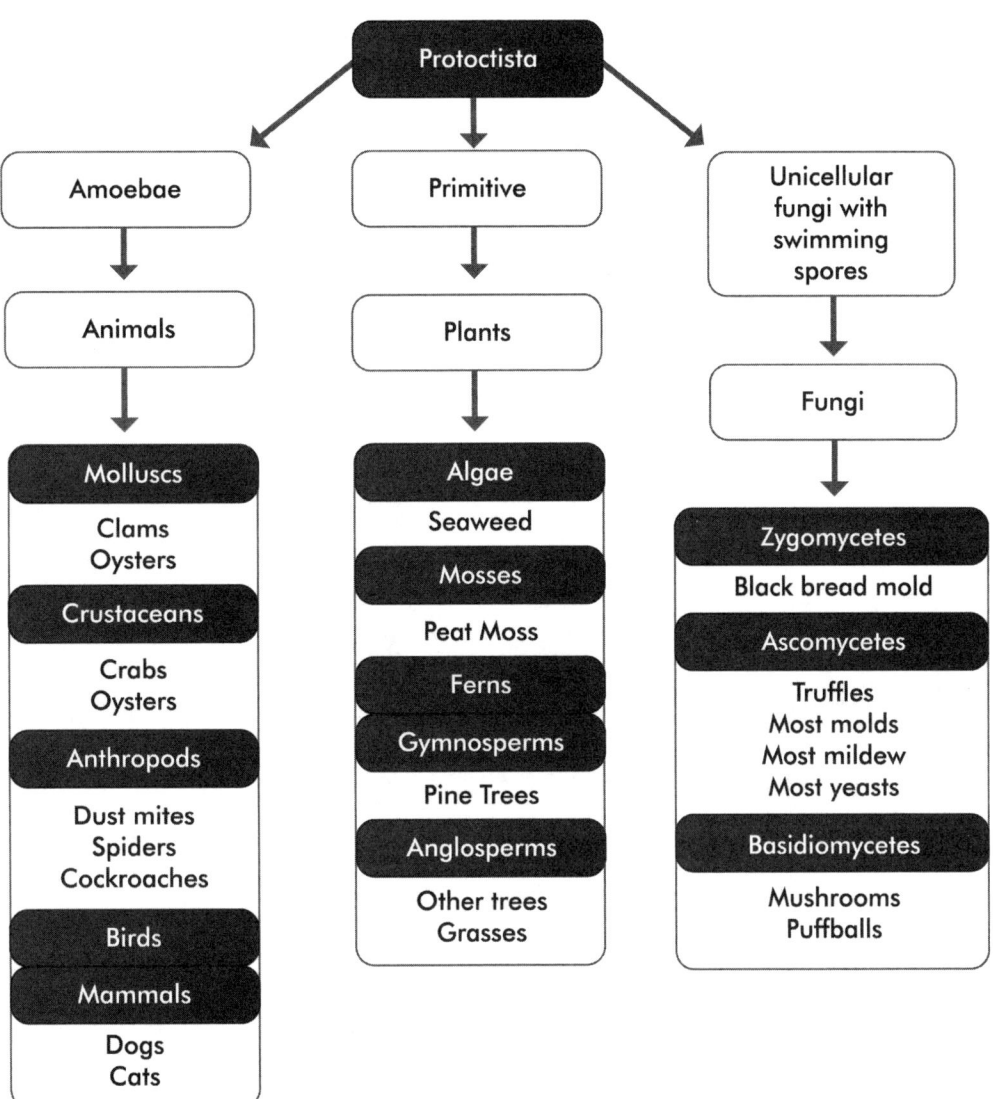

The diagram above demonstrates the role of fungi in relation to other living organisms. Fungi are not plants. Fungi are not animals. Fungi belong to a taxonomic classification, or kingdom, of their own. Plants convert carbon dioxide directly into carbohydrates for food. Animals and fungi must find complex carbon in the environment for food. While animals ingest the food and degrade it internally, fungi excrete chemicals (enzymes) into the environment that degrade the complex carbon into a soluble form.

Fungi do not make their own food the way that green plants do. Fungi get nourishment from other living organisms. The main role of fungi in the ecosystem is to break down dead materials, such as fallen leaves, trees, insects and animal carcasses. The same enzymes that assist fungi in breaking down dead materials are what help fungi to damage wooden components in a building. Molds can damage food, stored goods, and building materials of houses.

Yeast, mold, mildew and mushrooms are common forms of fungi. Mold is essentially a description of fungi that grows on surfaces, such as the black substance on a moldy shower wall. Mold and mildew often refer to the same type of fungi. All mold is fungi, but not all fungi is mold.

Molds grow in many colors, including white. "Black mold" is not a species or specific kind of mold, and neither is "toxic mold." Sometimes the news media use the terms "toxic mold" and "black mold" to refer to molds that may produce mycotoxins, or for a specific mold known as *Stachybotrys chartarum*. Molds that produce mycotoxins are often referred to as toxigenic fungi.

Molds can multiply by producing microscopic spores (2 to 100 microns [μm] in diameter), similar to the seeds produced by plants. Many spores are so small, they easily float through the air and can be carried for great distances by even the gentlest breeze. The number of mold spores suspended in indoor and outdoor air fluctuates from season to season, day to day, and even hour to hour.

No one knows how many species of fungi exist, but estimates range from the tens of thousands to perhaps 300,000 or more. Some of the more common indoor molds are *Penicillium, Aspergillus, Cladosporium* and *Alternaria*.

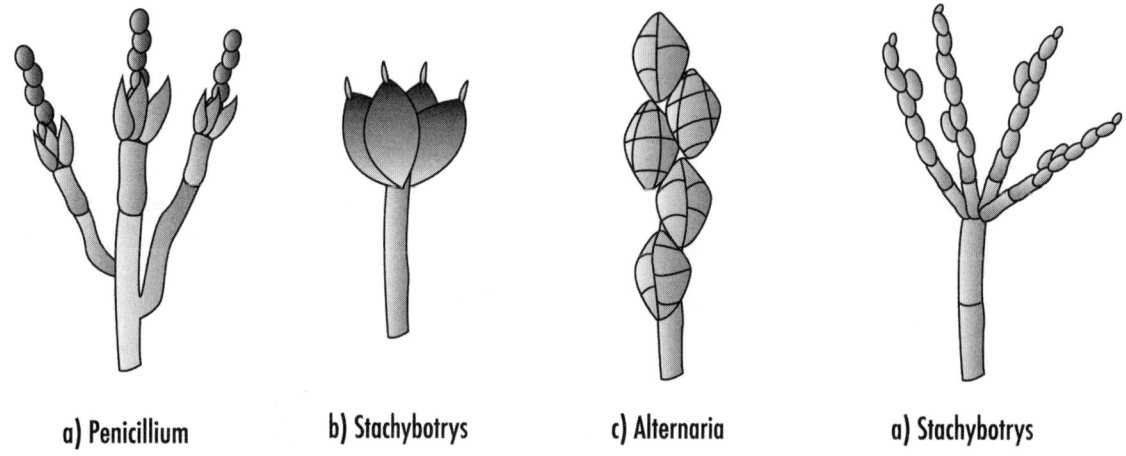

a) Penicillium   b) Stachybotrys   c) Alternaria   a) Stachybotrys

Mold Is Everywhere

Mold spores are ubiquitous; they are found both indoors and outdoors. Mold spores cannot be eliminated from indoor environments. Some mold spores will be found floating through the air and on settled dust; however, they will not grow if moisture is not present.

Why Be Concerned?

 Mold is not usually a problem indoors—unless mold spores land on a wet or damp spot and begin growing. As molds grow, they digest whatever they are growing on. Unchecked mold growth can damage buildings and furnishings; molds can rot wood, damage drywall, and eventually cause structural damage to buildings. Mold can cause cosmetic damage, such as stains, to furnishings. The potential human health effects of mold are also a concern. It is important, therefore, to prevent mold from growing indoors.

Discovering fungi in the indoor environment raises three major concerns:

1) the potential negative health effects of exposure to fungi and their byproducts;

2) the effects of fungal contamination on the structural integrity of a building; and

3) the negative aesthetic effects fungi can produce both visually and on the human olfactory system.

Although the issue of whether exposure to indoor fungi causes adverse health effects is controversial, there is no doubt that a seriously mold-contaminated building can suffer structural damage, and that a foul-smelling, fungus-filled building is aesthetically unpleasing. Controversies about health effects aside, the latter two reasons are sufficient to merit a Complete Mold Inspection and remediation when an environment is found to have fungal contamination.

People who have concerns about structural damage or the aesthetic effects of indoor fungi should seek the services of a certified mold inspector. People who have concerns about the health effects of mold exposure should seek the advice of a healthcare professional.

Section 4: Physical Characteristics of Mold

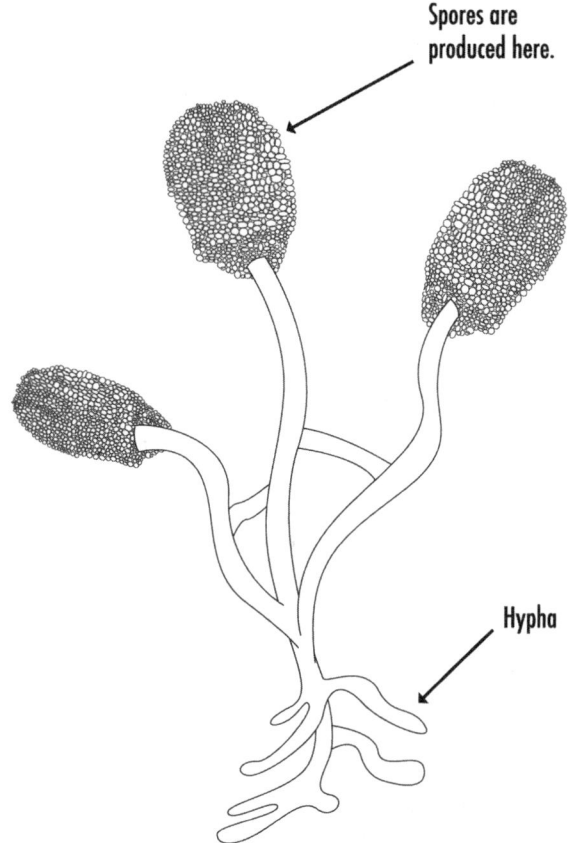

Spores are produced here.

Hypha

Molds are the most typical form of fungus found on Earth, comprising approximately 25% of the Earth's biomass.

Molds are made up of masses of thread-like cells called hyphae. Under the appropriate conditions, the hyphae will grow into long intertwining strings that form the main body of the fungus, or the mycelium. It is the mass of mycelium that is visible to the human eye.

Molds reproduce via seed-like spores present in the air and soil. However, molds can also spread if a fragment of broken hyphae is transplanted to an area with adequate moisture and organic matter for food. Spores are produced in large numbers. They are located on the hyphae.

A mass of hyphae, called a mycelium, is frequently visible on the surfaces of bread and wood. A mycelium often takes the shape of a fan or a fluffy mat. Mycelium is the intertwined mass of hyphae that forms the mold colony. The mycelium is also known as the body or thallus of the mold.

Vegetative mycelium is composed of those hyphae that adhere to the substrate and absorbs nutrients. Aerial mycelium is composed of those hyphae that grow up from the surface and support the spores.

In some molds, the lower hyphae will form small root-like structures called rhizoids. Rhizoids act like branched roots that help anchor the hyphae to the substrate or food source. Most of the mold body is buried in the food material (such as bread) and is out of sight. What is visible is the part of the mold body that produces spores.

The growth of fungi as hyphae on or in solid substrates is adapted for the efficient extraction of nutrients. Hyphae are specifically adapted for growth on solid surfaces and to invade substrates and tissues. They can exert large penetrative mechanical forces.

Some hyphae grow down into the food material. Cells of the hyphae can produce chemicals that break down the material (fruit, paper, wood) into nutrients that the fungus can absorb.

The structures of fungi vary widely. Some fungi have rigid cellular walls that are made of chitin. Chitin is resistant to breakdown as compared to the cellulose that makes up the cellular walls of plants. Spores can survive a very long time in harsh conditions until the environment is suitable for growth.

Fungi grow well in moist, dark areas, but can be found wherever organic material is available. Molds can grow on a variety of surfaces, including paint, jet fuel, wallpaper, glass and stainless steel. Moisture is necessary for mold growth. Moisture may come from the air and from the material

upon which mold grows. If the environment becomes very dry, fungi can survive by going dormant or by producing spores that resist drying out.

Fungi can spread via tiny spores through the air. When a spore lands upon a surface that is moist and has material that can be used for food, it germinates and begins to grow. Hyphae grow out of the spores. Some grow up to the air. Spores are produced on the hyphae that grow upward, above the food material. Spores can then be blown by the wind and spread to new areas.

A change in the humidity level can increase spores in the air. A high relative humidity (RH) can burst the moist, swollen cells of the mold body that form spores. This is true for *Penicillium* and *Aspergillus*, two common indoor molds. Foot traffic, vacuum cleaners, and increased ventilation can boost the number of airborne mold spores.

Quiz on Section 4

1. T/F: Molds are part of the kingdom Fungi.

    ☐ True
    ☐ False

2. The main role of fungi in the ecosystem is to _____.

    ☐ convert carbon dioxide
    ☐ produce spores
    ☐ produce mold and mildew
    ☐ ingest nutrients and degrade them internally
    ☐ grow mushrooms and truffles
    ☐ break down dead materials

3. T/F: All fungi is mold, but not all mold is fungi.

    ☐ True
    ☐ False

4. Two common types of indoor mold are *Penicilllium* and _____.

    ☐ *Claposdorium*
    ☐ *Aspergillus*
    ☐ *Asperinius*

5. People who have concerns about the health effects of mold exposure should _____.

    ☐ seek the advice of a healthcare professional
    ☐ hire a mold inspector
    ☐ hire a home inspector
    ☐ perform a mold sampling

6. A mold has like long, thread-like strings of cells called _____.

    ☐ hypthaelus
    ☐ hyphae
    ☐ hyptho

Answer Key is on page 149.

Section 5: Negative Health Effects and Mold

Topics Covered in This Section:

- Symptoms
- Infections
- Mycotoxins
- ODTS and HP
- PPE
- Contaminants

Inhalation exposure to mold indoors can cause negative health effects in some people. Molds produce allergens (substances that can cause allergic reactions), irritants and, in some cases, potentially toxic substances (mycotoxins). Inhaling or touching mold or mold spores may cause allergic reactions in sensitive individuals. Mold does not have to be alive to cause an allergic reaction in some people.

There are some specific groups of people who are potentially more easily or severely affected by mold than the average individual with no sensitivities to mold. They include infants, children, elderly people, individuals with respiratory conditions (such as allergies and asthma), and people with weakened immune systems (people with HIV/AIDS, chemotherapy patients, and organ transplant recipients).

Sensitive people should avoid areas that are likely to have mold, such as compost piles, cut grass and wooded areas.

Allergic reactions to mold in buildings do occur for many sensitive people. However, there is no conclusive evidence that proves that mold in a building directly causes illnesses in humans. More research is needed, and mold research has been continuous. Mold exposure as it relates to effects on human health is a complex and emerging science.

Symptoms of Mold Exposure

There are many symptoms of mold exposure. Current evidence indicates that allergies are the type of diseases most often associated with molds. An allergic reaction is the most common symptom, which could include wheezing and difficulty breathing.

According to the Centers for Disease Control, inhalation of fungal spores, fragments (parts), or metabolites (mycotoxins and volatile organic compounds) from a wide variety of fungi may lead to or exacerbate immunologic (allergic) reactions, cause toxic effects, or cause infections.

A single or repeated exposure to mold, mold spores, or mold fragments may cause non-sensitive individuals to become sensitive to mold, and repeated exposure has the potential to increase sensitivity. Allergic responses include "hay fever"-like symptoms, such as headache, sneezing, runny nose, irritated eyes, and skin rash (dermatitis). Molds can cause asthma attacks in people with asthma who are allergic to mold. Fungi in buildings may cause or exacerbate symptoms of allergies, especially in persons who have a history of allergic diseases (such as asthma and rhinitis). In addition, molds can irritate the eyes, skin, nose, throat and lungs of individuals, whether or not they are allergic to mold. Other symptoms include nasal and sinus congestion, burning, watery and red eyes, a sore throat, a dry cough, and skin irritation.

These and other symptoms may be associated with exposure to mold. But all of these symptoms may be caused by other exposures or conditions unrelated to mold growth. Therefore, it is important not to assume that mold is the cause of such symptoms.

The effects of mold exposure can be acute or chronic. An acute effect is an immediate, severe reaction to a large exposure. A chronic effect may take days, months or years to manifest, and usually comes from small, repeated exposures.

If a person experiences these symptoms only when occupying a particular building, then that person may possibly be experiencing symptoms of mold exposure.

There are four important indoor allergenic molds. They are *Penicillium, Aspergillus, Cladosporium* and *Alternaria. Alternaria* and *Cladosporium* are outdoor molds that can be found indoors if the doors or windows of a building are left open and the spores are carried in on air currents.

For more detailed information on mold and its health effects, consult a healthcare professional or the state or local health department.

Certified mold inspectors should not offer medical advice to clients. People with health problems that may be related to mold should seek a physician trained in occupational, environmental or allergy medicine. Recommend that clients may wish to consult with a healthcare provider regarding any health problems they might be experiencing.

Infections

Only a small group of fungi has been associated with infectious disease. Aspergillosis is an infectious disease that can occur in immune-suppressed persons. Health effects in this population can be severe. Several species of *Aspergillus* are known to cause aspergillosis. The most common is *Aspergillus fumigatus.* But exposure to this common mold, even to high concentrations, is unlikely to cause infection in a healthy person.

Breathing in mold may also cause hypersensitivity pneumonitis, an uncommon disease that resembles bacterial pneumonia. In addition, mold exposure may result in opportunistic infections in persons whose immune systems are weakened or suppressed.

There are fungal infections that can affect healthy people. There are pathogenic fungi sometimes found inside a building, such as: *Blastomyces* (which inhabit decaying wood); *Coccidioides* (found in the southwestern United States); *Cryptococcus* (found in bird droppings); and *Histoplasma* (found in bat guano or droppings). People without adequate personal protection equipment (PPE) who come in contact with bird or bat droppings, such as may be found in attics, could be at very high risk. People with compromised immune systems can be seriously affected by fungal infections.

Exposure to fungi associated with bird and bat droppings (*Histoplasma capsulatum* and *Cryptococcus neoformans*) can lead to negative health effects in healthy individuals, usually in the form of transient flu-like illnesses. Severe health effects are primarily encountered in immune-compromised persons. People with chronic lung illnesses, such as obstructive lung disease, may develop mold infections in their lungs.

Mycotoxins

As molds grow under some conditions, some (but not all) of them may produce potentially toxic byproducts called mycotoxins. Mycotoxins are fungal metabolites that have been identified as toxic agents. Some of these mycotoxin-producing molds are commonly found in moisture-damaged buildings. Exposure to mycotoxins can occur from inhalation, ingestion and skin contact. More than 200 mycotoxins from common molds have been identified, and many more remain to be identified. The amount and types of mycotoxins produced by a particular mold depends on many environmental and genetic factors.

No one can tell whether a mold is producing mycotoxins just by looking at it.

Many fungi, including species of *Aspergillus, Penicillium, Fusarium, Trichoderma, Memnoniella* and *Stachybotrys chartarum,* can produce potent mycotoxins, some of which are identical to the compounds produced by *Stachybotrys chartarum.*

There are studies that suggest an association between *Stachybotrys chartarum* and pulmonary hemorrhage/hemosiderosis in infants, generally those under 6 months old.

Mycotoxins can enter the human body through inhalation, ingestion or skin absorption. The effects of the toxic substance depend on the chemical or the material, the concentration, the route of entry, and the duration of exposure.

Smoking, alcohol, medication, gender, and existing health problems are all potential factors that can influence the effects of a toxic substance entering a body.

Some mycotoxins are known to affect people, but for many mycotoxins, little health information is available. Research on mycotoxins is ongoing.

ODTS and HP

Mold inspectors and mold remediators can be at risk of developing Organic Dust Toxic Syndrome (ODTS) or Hypersensitivity Pneumonitis (HP). ODTS may manifest itself with flu-like symptoms after a single, heavy exposure to dust contaminated with fungi. It differs from HP in that it is not an immune-mediated disease and does not require repeated exposures to the same causative agent. A variety of biological agents may cause ODTS, including common species of fungi. HP may occur after repeated exposures to an allergen and can result in permanent lung damage.

PPE

There have been reports linking negative health effects in office workers to offices contaminated with moldy surfaces, as well as symptoms in residents of homes contaminated with fungal growth. Fatigue, respiratory ailments, and eye irritation were typically observed in these cases.

Occupants and workers inside buildings can reduce their exposure by proper use of personal protective equipment (PPE), including respirators (minimum N-95), gloves, protective clothing, and goggles. Personal hygiene and habits are important for reducing exposure for remediation workers.

Contaminants

Although mold is frequently found in damp buildings, it is not the only potential contaminant. Biological contaminants other than mold, and non-biological contaminants, as well, are often present and may also cause negative health effects. Damp buildings may attract rodents and other pests. Damp or wet building components and furnishings may release chemicals indoors.

Potential contaminants in damp and wet buildings include bacteria, dust mites, cockroaches and other pests, as well as chemicals emitted by damp building materials and furnishings.

Quiz on Section 5

1. T/F: Dead or alive, mold can cause allergic reactions in some people.

    ☐ True
    ☐ False

2. T/F: Children are usually not affected by mold exposure more severely or sooner than other types of people.

    ☐ True
    ☐ False

3. Current evidence indicates that _____ are the types of disease most often associated with molds.

    ☐ migraines
    ☐ craniosynostoses
    ☐ erythroderma
    ☐ HIV
    ☐ arthrogryposis
    ☐ allergies

4. T/F: There are four important indoor allergenic molds. They are *Penicillium*, *Aspergillus*, *Cladosporium* and *Alternaria*.

    ☐ True
    ☐ False

5. As molds grow under certain conditions, some of them may produce potentially toxic byproducts called _____.

    ☐ micotoxins
    ☐ toxic mold
    ☐ mycotoxins
    ☐ mycotoxics
    ☐ mycleliums

6. T/F: Mold can cause asthma attacks.

    ☐ True
    ☐ False

Answer Key is on page 149.

Section 6: What Mold Needs to Grow

In previous sections, we learned what mold is. Now let's understand what mold needs to grow. That knowledge will help guide inspectors to the most likely locations in a building to find mold growth.

Most of the mold found indoors comes from the outdoors because mold spores can easily float on gentle air currents. If the spores land on suitable organic material inside a building, mold can begin to grow. But mold needs two things in order to grow and survive: moisture and food.

Moisture

Mold does not need a lot of moisture to grow. A little condensation in a bathroom or around a window sill, for example, can be enough. Common sites for indoor mold growth include bathroom tile and grout, basement walls, and areas around windows and sinks. Common sources of water or moisture include roof leaks, condensation due to high humidity or cold spots in a building, slow leaks at plumbing fixtures, humidification systems, sprinkler systems, and floods.

Mold has been found to germinate, grow and produce spores in as little as 24 hours after water damage occurs.

Indoor relative humidity (RH) should be between 20% and 40% in the winter, and less than 60% the rest of the year. Some experts recommended that indoor humidity levels in general should be between 40% and 60%.

Moisture is the most important factor influencing mold growth indoors. Controlling indoor moisture helps limit mold growth. Moisture control is the key to mold control.

Food

Besides moisture, mold needs nutrients, or food, to grow. Mold can grow on virtually any organic substance. Buildings are full of organic materials that mold can use as food, including paper, cloth, wood, plant material, and even soil. Molds secrete digestive enzymes that decompose the substrate, making nutrients available. Some molds can even digest synthetic materials, such as adhesives, pastes and paints.

Molds can also grow on inorganic material, such as concrete, glass and metal, because they can grow on the dirt or dust that is present on the surfaces of those materials.

In most cases, temperature is not an issue; some molds grow in warm areas, while others prefer cool locations, such as bread stored in a refrigerator.

Mold grows well in environments between 40° to 100° F. (And the pH is usually between 3 and 8.) But some mold species have been found in hot springs with water temperatures above 120° F.

Often, more than one type of mold can be found growing in the same area, although conditions such as moisture, substrate and temperature may favor one species of mold over another.

Section 7: Building Science and Mold

Building Science in Relation to Moisture and Microbial Growth

Micro-organisms can be found in the air inside a building, on a surface inside a building (on the floor, ceiling, walls and furniture), and inside the HVAC system of a building. Many of these micro-organisms come indoors from outside. They come from decaying organic matter or moist earth.

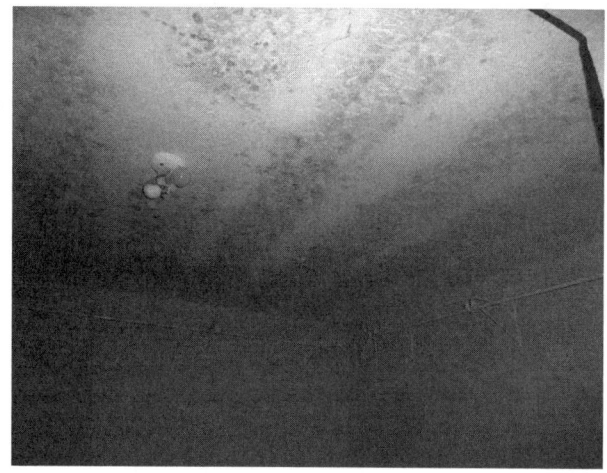

Micro-organisms can enter a building by floating with outdoor air that enters the building, or they can travel on people and animals who bring them inside.

Micro-organisms might be present on the building materials as the structure is being constructed. Oftentimes, inspectors will find building materials lying on the ground at a new construction site. These materials absorb moisture and dirt and may support mold growth inside the building, after construction has been completed.

Mold growth is not desirable in a building and must be prevented. There are three reasons to prevent fungal growth inside a building: the potential negative health effects of exposure to fungi and their byproducts; the effects of mold contamination on the structural integrity of the building; and the negative aesthetic effects fungi can produce, both visually and on the human olfactory system.

Moisture, Temperature, Food and Time

There are four factors involved in mold growth. The following conditions are necessary for mold growth to thrive on surfaces:

- a temperature range between 40° and 100° F;
- the presence of mold spores;
- a nutrient base (most surfaces contain nutrients); and
- moisture.

Human comfort constraints limit the practical ability to control temperature in the growth of mold. Air temperature inside a building that is suitable for occupants is also beneficial for mold growth. Most buildings are kept between 65° and 75° F, and this temperature range is also suitable for mold to grow, although some fungi can thrive in temperatures as cold as 15° F and as hot as 122° F.

Spores are almost always present in outdoor and indoor air. Almost all construction materials and furnishings can provide nutrients to support mold growth, and dirt on surfaces provides additional nutrients. It is virtually impossible to eliminate all nutrients. A building is filled with an abundant supply of food for mold growth. Fungi have been shown to colonize on drywall, wood paneling, wallpaper, ceiling tiles, carpeting and pads, furniture, insulated ductwork, and other building components. The fungi break down the materials for food or use the dust that has collected on a surface as a nutrient source.

Temperature, food and time cannot be adequately manipulated to control microbial growth, but moisture can. Moisture is the controlling factor. Therefore, moisture control is the primary strategy to focus on in order to limit and prevent mold growth. Once moisture intrusion into a building takes place, mold can start growing in very little time. Fungi have been shown to be capable of germination, growth and sporulation in as little as 24 hours after water intrusion or damage occurs.

Building Science

To understand how to find mold and prevent its growth in a building, inspectors must study and understand building science. Building science, in relation to mold, is the study of the building's dynamics as affected by moisture intrusion. Buildings are dynamic environments influenced by geographic location, season, weather conditions, the HVAC's system design and operation, moisture intrusion, pest colonization, and human activities. Building dynamics continually change and affect the conditions for mold growth.

Moisture Content

Moisture content (MC) is often expressed as a percentage $(100 \times (\text{wet mass} - \text{dry mass})) \div (\text{dry mass})$, or in terms of the amount of water in a certain volume (lbs./ft. cubed).

Mold requires moisture to survive, so protecting lumber and wood structures from moisture will help prevent mold growth. Mold growth can be limited if the MC of wood can be kept below 20%. An MC below 17% means that virtually no microbial growth will occur on even the most susceptible materials. Southern pine dimensional lumber is typically kiln-dried to a maximum 19% MC or less. The moisture content is indicated on the grade stamp. Moisture content is related directly to particular substrates or materials. Microbial growth is limited when the MC of gypsum board is below 0.6%, when brick is below 0.8%, when wallpaper is below 10.5%, and when concrete is below 5%. One study showed that a moisture content greater than 5% permitted the growth of *Penicillium glabrum* and *Aspergillus versicolor* on ceiling tiles in a laboratory.

Mold growth does not require the presence of standing water; it can occur when high relative humidity or the hygroscopic properties (the tendency to absorb and retain moisture) of building surfaces allow sufficient moisture to accumulate. Relative humidity and the factors that govern it are often misunderstood. This section is intended to give building inspectors an understanding of the factors that govern relative humidity, and to describe common moisture problems and their solutions.

Relative Humidity

Understanding relative humidity in a building is essential to controlling mold growth. Relative humidity (RH) is a ratio (expressed as a percentage) of the amount of moisture in the air to the maximum amount of moisture the air can hold. Warm air can hold more moisture than cool air. RH is a factor in determining how much moisture is present in a room, but it is the available moisture in a substrate (not the RH of the room's air) that determines if mold can grow or not.

Many sources recommend maintaining RH in living spaces below 60% to limit microbial growth. By keeping RH below 60%, one may assume that the moisture content in building materials would be low. However, this assumption may be false because mold grows on surfaces and in building materials, not in the air. Therefore, it is the RH in the air adjacent to the surface, not the ambient RH, that must be lowered in order to control mold growth. Measuring a room with an RH at or below 60% may mean that the building materials are fairly dry, but it does not eliminate the possibility of mold growth because local cold spots and water intrusion may allow the RH of the air adjacent to the surface to exceed 70%.

Moisture meters are essential for inspectors; they enable inspectors to identify damp areas that would otherwise not be evident. Infrared cameras are praised for their ability to detect moisture that is not readily visible.

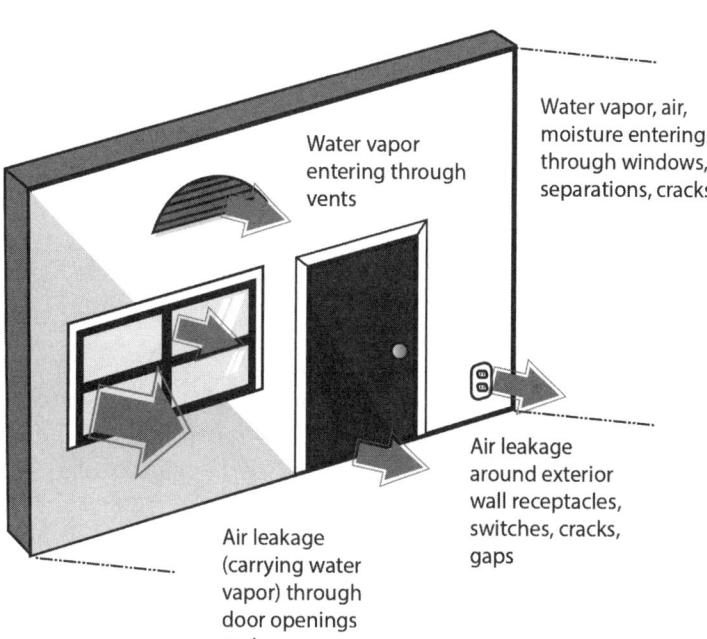

Water vapor entering through vents

Water vapor, air, moisture entering through windows, separations, cracks

Air leakage around exterior wall receptacles, switches, cracks, gaps

Air leakage (carrying water vapor) through door openings and gaps

Water enters buildings both as a liquid and as a gas (water vapor). Water, in its liquid form, is introduced intentionally in bathrooms, kitchens and laundries, but accidentally by way of leaks and spills. Some of that water evaporates and joins the water vapor that is exhaled by building occupants as they breathe, or that which is introduced by humidifiers. Water vapor also moves in and out of the building as part of the air that is mechanically introduced or that infiltrates and exfiltrates through openings in the building's shell.

A lesser amount of water vapor diffuses into and out of the building through the building materials themselves.

The sketch above illustrates the usual locations of moisture entry, and how all those entry paths can add to the moisture gain of the building.

The ability of air to hold water vapor decreases as the air temperature is lowered. If a unit of air contains half of the water vapor it can hold, it is said to be at 50% relative humidity (RH). As the air cools, the relative humidity increases. RH rises as the air cools because cooler air has a lower moisture-holding capacity, increasing the risk of condensation in walls.

If the air contains all of the water vapor it can hold, it is at 100% RH, and the water vapor condenses, changing from a gas to a liquid. It is possible to reach 100% RH without changing the amount of water vapor in the air (its vapor pressure or absolute humidity); all that is required is for the air temperature to drop to the dew point.

Relative humidity and temperature often vary within a room, while the absolute humidity in the room's air can usually be assumed to be uniform. Therefore, if one side of the room is warm and the other side is cool, the cool side of the room has a higher RH than the warm side.

The highest RH in a room is always next to the coldest surface. This is referred as the "first condensing surface," as it will be the location where condensation first occurs if the relative humidity at the surface reaches 100%. It is important to understand this when trying to understand why mold is growing on one patch of wall or only along the wall-ceiling joint. It is likely that the surface of the wall is cooler than the room's ambient air because there is a void in the insulation, or because wind is blowing through cracks in the exterior of the building.

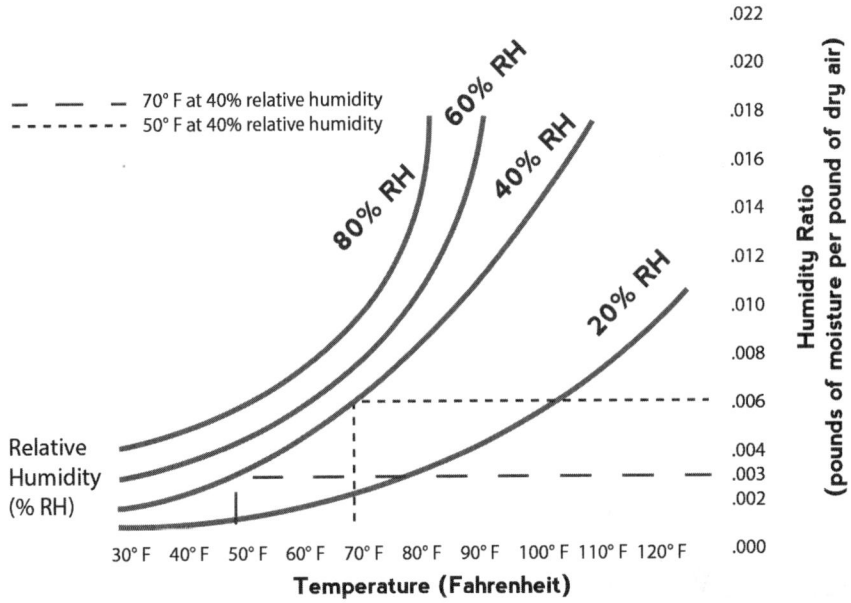

The chart above showing the relative humidity reading taken in a room will only give an accurate indication of the actual amount of moisture present if a temperature reading is taken at the same time. The chart shows that air at 70° F and 40% RH contains approximately 0.006 pounds of moisture per pound of dry air (as indicated by the bold line), while air that is at 50° F and 40% RH contains approximately 0.003 pounds of moisture per pound of dry air (as indicated by the dashed line). Although both are at 40% RH, the 70° F air contains roughly twice as much moisture as the 50° F air.

Condensation in Cold Climates

The basic idea in controlling condensation due to vapor migration is to prevent warm, moisture-laden air from contacting cool surfaces. In cold climates, condensation can occur within an exterior wall of a building when warm, moist indoor air flows outward. This warm, moist air cools as it nears the outer boundary of the exterior wall.

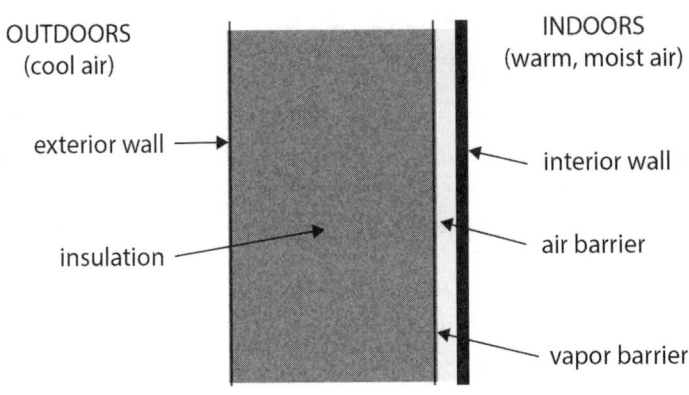

RH rises as the air cools because cooler air has a lower moisture-holding capacity, which increases the potential for condensation forming in the walls.

To control condensation in a building's exterior walls in cold climates:

- Install insulation to prevent large temperature differences between the air and surfaces.

- Install air or vapor barriers on the warm side of the building envelope.

- Use ventilation to reduce indoor moisture levels below levels that allow condensation to occur.

Condensation in Hot and Humid Climates

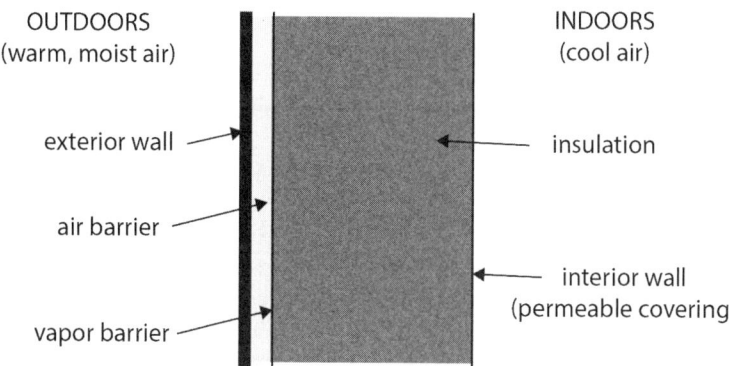

To control condensation in a building's exterior walls in hot, humid climates:

- Install insulation to prevent large temperature differences between the air and surfaces.

- Install air or vapor barriers on the exterior-side of the building envelope.

- Avoid impermeable vinyl or other wall coverings, and use permeable paints and wall coverings on the interior surfaces of the exterior walls.

- The HVAC system should be producing net-positive pressures on the inside of the building, with respect to the outdoors, to avoid entry of outdoor air inward.

- Try to avoid cooling interior spaces below the average monthly outdoor dew-point temperature for the climate where the building is located. In some areas, this may not be possible.

Many buildings incorporate vapor barriers in the design of their walls and floors. Vapor barriers must be located and installed properly or the building may develop moisture problems. A vapor barrier is a layer of material that slows or prevents the absorption or release of moisture from or into a wall or floor. Vapor barriers can prevent damp or wet building materials from drying quickly enough, which may allow mold growth.

Humidifiers

Moisture from humidifiers may support microbial growth on wet surfaces where moisture can condense during cold weather. Humidifiers that discharge small droplets of water from a reservoir are prone to supporting mold growth. Moisture accumulation inside dirty ductwork creates a suitable environment for mold growth. The reservoir of the humidifier is usually contaminated to some degree. Humidifiers should be considered potential sources for mold growth.

Windows

In winter, windows are typically the coldest surfaces in a room. The interior surface of a window is often the first condensing surface in a room. Condensation on window surfaces has historically been controlled by using storm windows or insulated glass to raise interior surface temperatures. The advent of high-performance glazing systems has led to a greater incidence of moisture problems in heating climate-controlled building enclosures because the buildings can now be operated at higher interior vapor pressures (or moisture levels) without visible surface condensation on windows. In older building enclosures with less advanced glazing systems, visible condensation on the windows can alert the occupants to the need for ventilation to flush out interior moisture (such as by opening the windows).

RH and Temperature

Mold is often found on the exterior wall surfaces of corner rooms in cold climates. An exposed corner room is likely to be significantly colder than adjoining rooms, so it has a higher relative humidity (RH) than other rooms at the same water-vapor pressure. If mold growth is found in a corner room, then relative humidity levels next to the room's surfaces are above 70%. However, is the RH above 70% at the surfaces because the room is too cold, or because there is too much moisture present (or high water-vapor pressure)?

The amount of moisture in the room can be estimated by measuring both temperature and RH at the same location at the same time. Suppose there are two cases: In the first case, assume that the RH is 30% and the temperature is 70° F in the middle of the room. The low RH at that temperature indicates that the water-vapor pressure (or absolute humidity) is low. The high surface-RH is probably due to room surfaces that are "too cold." Temperature is the dominant factor, and control strategies should involve increasing the temperature at cold room surfaces.

In the second case, assume that the RH is 50% and the temperature is 70° F in the middle of the room. The higher RH at that temperature indicates that the water-vapor pressure is high, and there is a relatively large amount of moisture in the air. The high surface-RH is probably due to air that is "too damp." Humidity is the dominant factor, and control strategies should involve decreasing the moisture content of the indoor air.

Quiz on Section 7

1. A(n) _____ contains an abundant supply of nutrients for mold growth.

    ☐ building

    ☐ bathroom

    ☐ freezer of food

2. Once a building is affected by _____, mold can start growing in very little time.

    ☐ soot and dirt particles

    ☐ air infiltration

    ☐ human traffic

    ☐ humidity movement

    ☐ moisture intrusion

    ☐ biocide usage

3. _____, in relation to mold, is the study of the building's dynamics as affected by moisture intrusion.

    ☐ Home inspections

    ☐ Building science

    ☐ Mathematics

    ☐ Molecular biology

    ☐ Micro-organisms

    ☐ Chemistry

4. Mold growth can be limited if the MC of wood can be kept below ____. Below a ____ MC of wood, virtually no microbial growth will occur on even the most susceptible materials.

    ☐ 35%..... 45%

    ☐ 24%..... 20%

    ☐ 17%..... 22%

    ☐ 10%..... 50%

    ☐ 20%.....17%

5. T/F: RH is a factor in determining how much moisture is present in a room, but it is the available moisture in a substrate (not the RH of the room's air) that determines if mold can grow or not.

    ☐ True

    ☐ False

6. T/F: To control condensation in a building's exterior walls in cold climates, install air or vapor barriers on the warm side of the building's envelope.

☐ True
☐ False

7. T/F: Humidifiers should be considered potential sources of mold growth.

☐ True
☐ False

Answer Key is on page 149.

Section 8: Finding Mold in Buildings

We know what mold is, and we know what mold needs to grow. Now let's learn how and where to find mold in a building.

A building can become a perfect place for mold growth when the building has construction flaws, systems or components that are damaged or inoperable, or experiences delayed maintenance. Any part of a building that facilitates the entry of moisture into its materials creates the potential for mold growth. Wooden components, drywall, carpeting, plaster, wallpaper, and many other building materials provide fertile conditions for mold growth when they become wet. Water-damaged materials provide optimum sites for mold growth.

About a third of all homes in the United States experience some type of water damage every year. Where there is water damage, there may be mold growth. When a home has mold growth, addressing the problem can create an additional financial burden, not to mention some potentially serious health risks.

Use Your Eyes

A visual inspection is the most important first step in identifying possible mold contamination.

A certified mold inspection includes a non-invasive, visual examination of the readily accessible, visible, and installed systems and components listed in the IAC2 Mold Inspection Standards of Practice, as well as at least one sampling for mold growth, according to the IAC2 Mold Sampling Procedures.

The inspector shall report moisture intrusion, water damage, musty odors, apparent mold growth, and conditions conducive to mold growth.

Look for mold growth, which may appear cottony, velvety, granular or leathery, and have varied colors of white, gray, brown, black, yellow and/or green. Mold often appears as a discoloration, staining, or fuzzy growth on the surface of building materials and furnishings.

General Guide to Performing an Examination:

- Check the general grading of the ground around the perimeter of the building. Look for unusual or problematic conditions. The ground should be sloped away from the building.

- Examine the downspouts and discharge of the roof water. Examine storm water collection systems. Examine swales or drainage areas, and drainage systems. There should be no standing water for more than 12 hours after a rainstorm.

- The exterior siding materials and building envelope should be inspected carefully. Flashing details should be secure. Trim around windows and doors should be watertight. Check the condition of the sealant. Inspect for weep holes where required. Note the condition of the siding and trim.

- The roof system shall be inspected carefully. Check for damaged, worn or deteriorated areas. Flashing should be installed securely. Look for patching and repairs.

- Inside the building, check the walls, ceilings and floors. Pay attention to painted surfaces. Look for patching and repairs. Look for water stains and watermarks. Note any odors. Measure the humidity levels. Measure for wet, damp and moist areas.

- Inspect the bathrooms and toilet rooms. Run water at all the fixtures. Check for water leaks and signs of prior water leaks and repairs. Check the exhaust fans and the locations where they discharge. Check for microbial growth around the bathroom vent fans, the toilet, and inside the sink/vanity cabinet. Bathroom carpeting can also support mold growth.

- In the kitchen, all the appliances and fixtures should be operated and inspected. Look for water stains and leaks under the sinks inside the cabinets. Check the area inside the sink cabinet for microbial growth. Check for water dripping from the dishwasher or refrigerator. The exhaust fan should be discharging outside. Check the area around the exhaust fan and the filtering system for microbial growth.

- Check humidifiers for mold. Note the method of how any dehumidifier is discharging the collected water.

- Inspect condensation or drip pans underneath air-conditioning coils. Mold is often found on the coil fins themselves. There should not be standing water in any collection pans.

- Enter crawlspaces and check for humidity and moisture. Ventilation and insulation problems often support mold growth in under-floor crawlspaces. Exposed dirt floors should be sealed with a vapor barrier. Check for condensation on plumbing pipes and un-insulated ductwork passing through non-conditioned spaces.

- Basements should be inspected for moisture intrusion and water penetration problems, as well as actual water damage. Check for efflorescence on masonry walls. Carpeting an un-insulated concrete floor is not recommended. Check sump pumps and their discharge. Check perimeter drainage channels or trenches.

- Check for leaks and condensation at all visible plumbing pipes and lines. Check the hot water source for leaks, drips and discharge.

- Examine the fire sprinkler system, including its valves, pipes and sprinkler heads, for leaks and drips.

- Enter and examine accessible attic spaces. Check for properly installed and adequate ventilation and insulation.

- Examine enclosed structures around spas, whirlpools, swimming pools, saunas and other areas with high humidity levels.

- Check the clothes dryer exhaust vents.

- Examine the proper ventilation of the exhaust of all combustion appliances, including the fuel-fired heating system and hot water source.

Smell for Odors

Search for areas of noticeable musty odors. Even if you can't see mold, you may suspect hidden mold if you know there has been a water problem in the building, and especially if its occupants are reporting health problems.

Some compounds produced by molds have strong smells and are volatile and quickly released into the air. These compounds are known as microbial volatile organic compounds (mVOCs), which are small molecules that don't tend to settle on carpeting or other surfaces, as mold spores do. They can pass through walls and spread throughout the inside of buildings. However, like mycotoxins and enzymes, they can't be transmitted very far outdoors when exposed to sunlight. Therefore, their presence inside of buildings is direct evidence of active or recently active mold growth.

Because mVOCs often have strong or unpleasant odors, they can be the source of the moldy odor or musty smell frequently associated with mold growth. A moldy odor suggests that mold is growing in the building and should be investigated. The health effects of inhaling mVOCs are largely unknown, although exposure to mVOCs has been linked to symptoms such as headaches, nasal irritation, dizziness, fatigue and nausea. More research is needed to determine whether there are any human health effects from non-occupational indoor exposures to mVOCs.

Check for Conducive Conditions

A visual examination of a building includes reporting conditions conducive to mold growth. The following is a list of such conditions. This list is for informational purposes only and is not all-inclusive. Certain physical conditions may exist at a property that are not listed, and certain activities or procedures that are beyond the scope of a standard inspection may be warranted, to be recommended at the discretion of the inspector.

Some conditions conducive to mold growth include:

- defects in systems or components that may allow water or moisture penetration;
- evidence of flooding;
- water damage;
- water stains;
- standing water or puddles;
- indoor surfaces that are too cold;
- carpeting that was wet;
- house plants (watering them can generate large amounts of moisture);
- over-watering of potted plants;
- indoor humidity that is too high;
- the use of a humidifier;
- steam radiators;
- line-drying the laundry indoors;
- firewood stored indoors;
- condensation problems;
- condensing moisture on air-conditioning ducts and windowpanes;
- negative grading;
- water inside a perimeter-drainage channel;
- irrigation sprinkler systems that are not spraying efficiently;
- downspouts not discharging far enough away from the building;
- clogged or inoperative gutter system;

- leaking gutters;

- improperly installed flashing;

- deteriorated condition of the roof covering;

- roof leaks;

- missing vapor barrier;

- plumbing system leaks, or defects in appliances, such as a leaking dishwasher;

- loosely secured toilets with leaking wax rings or seals;

- overflow of water from tubs, sinks or toilets;

- water inside a sump pump bucket;

- dripping water valves;

- improper or inadequate discharge of exhaust from the clothes dryer, bath vent or kitchen fan;

- improper venting of combustion appliances;

- a dirty air filter or a clogged condensate drainage in the HVAC system;

- failure to vent the clothes dryer exhaust to the outdoors (including electric dryers);

- non-insulated ductwork inside an unconditioned space;

- inadequately ventilated spaces, such as an attic space with its vents blocked by insulation;

- crawlspaces with exposed dirt floors;

- moisture movement through basement walls and slab;

- water or moisture intrusion at carpeting in the corner of a below-grade basement;

- a fire-suppression sprinkler head that is dripping water; and

- any building system or component that may contribute to a moisture problem.

Ask Occupants

You may suspect hidden mold if you know there has been a water problem in the building and its occupants are reporting health problems. If the building's occupants complain about noticeable odors, musty smells, or elevated humidity levels in any room of the building, there may exist conditions favorable to mold growth. If residents relate experiencing allergic reactions or symptoms in a particular area of the building, mold growth may be present.

Check for Moisture Intrusion

Moisture intrusion includes groundwater intrusion, surface water intrusion, water intrusion originating from inside the building (such as from a plumbing leak), and condensation.

Look for active moisture intrusion into the building. Look for signs of excess moisture or water damage. Sampling for mold is recommended if water or moisture penetration is visually evident during an examination.

A moisture meter shall be used during a mold inspection. There are many different types of moisture meters. Even the most basic one is essential to conducting a Complete Mold Inspection. Moisture meters can provide qualitative information, but may not indicate the actual amount of water available to micro-organisms for growth.

Moisture measurements should be taken in every room and area of concern in the building.

Moisture problems can have many causes. Some have been linked to changes in building construction practices since the 1970s. These practices led to constructing buildings that are tightly sealed but, in some cases, lack adequate ventilation. Without adequate ventilation, moisture may build up indoors and enable mold to grow.

A building must be properly designed for climate, site location and use, and its design must be strictly followed during construction, or the building may wind up with moisture-control problems.

Delayed or insufficient maintenance can also lead to moisture problems in buildings. Undiscovered or ignored moisture problems can create an environment conducive to mold growth. Moisture problems in temporary structures, such as portable classrooms, are also frequently associated with mold problems.

Common moisture problems include:

- leaking roofs;

- leaking or condensation on water pipes, especially pipes inside wall cavities or pipe chases;

- leaking fire-protection sprinkler systems;

- landscaping, gutters and/or downspouts that direct water into or under a building;

- high humidity (greater than 60% relative humidity);

- unvented combustion appliances, such as clothes dryers vented into a garage (clothes dryers and other combustion appliances should be vented to the outdoors); and

- under-floor crawlspaces with an exposed dirt floor.

Some moisture problems are not easy to see. For example, the interiors of walls where pipes and wires are run (pipe chases and utility tunnels) are common sites of mold growth. Mold is frequently found on walls in cold corners and behind furniture where condensation can form.

Other potential locations of hidden moisture, resulting in hidden mold growth, include:

- poorly draining condensate drain pans inside air-handling units;

- porous thermal or acoustic liners inside ductwork;

- roof materials above ceiling tiles;

- the backside of drywall (also known as gypsum board, wallboard or Sheetrock®) or paneling;

- under carpeting and pads;

- behind wallpaper;

- under vinyl flooring;

- inside sink cabinets;

- under furniture; and

- behind stored items placed near an exterior wall or on a cold floor.

Condensation Inside HVAC Ducts

An increase (up to 90%) in the relative humidity of air downstream of cooling coils is a natural result of the energy transfer between the air and the coils. Moisture may condense on cool surfaces in contact with this damp air or may wick off cooling coils. Particles such as soil, organic matter, and micro-organisms that are not removed by the filter system can collect on surfaces within HVAC systems. Such organic matter may support microbial growth under wet or damp conditions. Inspectors should sample surfaces inside HVAC systems if microbial growth is suspected and needs to be confirmed. Any surfaces within supply air ducts that can accumulate dirt can be a place for mold growth, if adequate moisture is present.

Humidifiers

Reservoirs for humidification devices that use re-circulated cold water are always microbially contaminated, to some degree. They should always be considered potential sources for mold.

Check Humidity

Relative humidity (RH) measurements should be taken in all areas of the building that have conditions that have led to moisture intrusion, water damage, musty odors, apparent mold growth, or conditions conducive to mold growth.

Sometimes, humidity or dampness in the air (water vapor) can supply enough moisture for mold growth. Indoor relative humidity (RH) should be kept below 60% and, ideally, between 30% and 50%.

Low humidity may also discourage pests, such as cockroaches and dust mites.

Humidity levels can rise in a building as the result of the use of humidifiers, steam radiators, moisture-generating appliances (such as dryers), and combustion appliances (such as stoves). Cooking and showering can also add to indoor humidity.

One function of the building's heating, ventilation and air-conditioning (HVAC) system is to remove moisture from the air before the air is distributed throughout the building. If the HVAC system is turned off during or shortly after major cleaning efforts that involve a lot of water (such as mopping and carpet shampooing), the humidity may rise significantly, and moisture or mold problems may develop.

Condensation can be a sign of high humidity. When warm, humid air contacts a cold surface, condensation may form. (To see this, remove a cold bottle of water from a refrigerator and take it outside on a hot day. Typically, condensation will form on the outside of the bottle.)

Intrusion of humid outdoor air could result in chronic condensation on windows, perimeter walls, and other cool surfaces.

Humidity can be measured with a humidity gauge or meter. There are models available that can monitor both temperature and humidity.

Check Temperature

In all areas where there is moisture intrusion, water damage, apparent mold growth, musty odors, and/or conditions conducive to mold growth, the inspector should take temperature measurements. Mold tends to grow well in temperatures ranging from 32° to 104° F.

Hidden Problems

In most cases, finding indoor mold growth may not be easy. Mold does not need light to grow; it can grow in dark areas and on hidden surfaces, such as the backside of drywall, wallpaper and paneling, on the top-side of ceiling tiles, and on the underside of carpets and pads. Possible locations of hidden mold also include damp areas behind walls and in crawlspaces, inside pipe chases and utility tunnels (areas inside walls where water and other pipes are run), on acoustic liners in ventilation ducts, and on roof materials above ceiling tiles.

Investigating for hidden mold can be difficult. It requires a professional with experience in inspecting for water and moisture problems. A certified home inspector is best qualified to perform a thorough mold inspection. Certified home inspectors are trained to locate and identify moisture intrusion, condensation, and humidity problems. Certified home inspectors are trained in building science, which is required to investigate moisture intrusion and conditions conducive to mold growth. (For information about training to become a certified home inspector, visit **www.nachi.org**.)

Investigating hidden mold requires caution, since disturbing moldy areas may spread mold throughout the building. Operating air handlers, for example, can send high levels of dust and mold into the air to circulate throughout the building.

Personal protective equipment (PPE) is not always needed when looking for mold, but it should always be available. If a potential exists for mold to be released into the air, inspectors should use PPE to reduce exposure.

Maintenance Personnel of Large Buildings

A key step in looking for mold in a building is to determine whether there has been a water leak. Maintenance personnel are frequently among the first to know when moisture problems have occurred. In some cases, management or health and safety personnel will have been notified. Touring the building with maintenance or other personnel involved with the water problem may be helpful.

Inspect Crawlspaces

Under-floor crawlspaces should be included in an inspection of a building. A white, fibrous material on the soil of the crawlspace may indicate alkaline salts and not mold, but may still suggest that moisture has been a problem. The inspector should recommend that the area be more extensively investigated.

Crawlspaces are common sites of hidden mold growth, particularly if they have bare earth floors, since relative humidity (RH) in these locations can be high. The soil will wick moisture, through capillary action, from damp to dry areas. The relative warmth of the crawlspace will dry the soil by evaporation, adding this moisture to the air in the crawlspace, where it can cause mold to grow. Also, in areas where the water table is high and weather conditions are suitable, groundwater may enter a crawlspace.

The moisture that accumulates in a crawlspace may also enter another part of the building and contribute to mold growth there. Moisture can pass from a crawlspace into a building through cracks in walls, floors and ceilings. Crawlspaces should be designed specifically to avoid moisture problems.

Keep in mind that mold levels in confined spaces, such as crawlspaces, are likely to be high, so PPE should be used accordingly.

Inspect HVAC

The building's air-handling system should be inspected to determine whether it is moldy. Moisture may collect in the ventilation system due to poor condensate pan drainage, poor roof drainage, or high humidity in the ventilation ducts. In some cases, water may enter the ventilation ducts from a leaky pipe. A contaminated ventilation system may spread mold spores throughout the building, and should be considered a high priority for investigation and repair. Mold contamination in the ventilation system should be mitigated as soon as possible in a manner that does not expose the building's occupants to dust and mold spores.

Filters may become damp during the air-conditioning season. Micro-organisms may grow on a damp filter or on collected dust. Mold sampling of the material accumulated on the filter may distinguish between a normal accumulation of material of biological origin on a filter and actual microbial growth.

Mold growing near the intake to an HVAC system likely indicates ventilation humidity problems. An HVAC system that is part of an identified moisture problem may also be a site of mold growth. Experience and professional judgment should be used when working with the HVAC system; consult a professional, if needed.

If the HVAC system has insulation on the inside of the air ducts, and the insulation gets wet or moldy, it should be removed and replaced because the material cannot be cleaned sufficiently.

Look for:

- standing water under the cooling coils of air handlers;
- condensate pans that could have excess water in them;
- drain pans that slope toward the drain (the drain should be flowing freely);
- ducts are that are properly sealed and insulated in all non-air-conditioned spaces so that moisture due to condensation does not enter the system, so that the system works as intended. To prevent condensation, the heating and cooling system must be properly insulated;
- proper installation and maintenance of any in-duct humidification equipment, according to the manufacturer's recommendations;
- dampness of the filters, which can lead to microbial growth;
- dirty cooling coils, which are conducive to microbial growth;
- dampness and microbial growth on the acoustical lining;
- poorly maintained humidifier units with stagnant water; and
- surface deposits, rust or microbial growth on the air supply registers.

Return-Air Registers

Mold spores that are released in one room of a residential building may be circulated to other parts of the building. The mold spores may settle on dirt or dust that is located anywhere in the duct system through which the air travels. These spores could become moistened by the circulating air, especially if there is a humidifier operating in the building. An inspector should check the return-air registers for indications of visible mold growth. A lack of maintenance and cleaning of the ducts can be a reason for suspecting microbial growth inside the ductwork.

Consult the EPA's guide titled "Should You Have the Air Ducts in Your Home Cleaned?" Although this publication focuses on ducts in homes, the information it contains is applicable to other building types.

A window air conditioner could have a dirty filter or grille. There could be standing water inside the unit. There could be moisture dripping from the bottom of a window unit, as evidenced by moisture damage at the bottom corners of the window opening or directly below the unit.

Check the Structure

Molds gradually destroy whatever they grow on, so preventing mold growth also prevents damage to building materials and furnishings. If a mold or moisture problem goes unaddressed long enough, structural damage is likely to result. For example, if a roof is allowed to leak long enough, mold can weaken floors and walls by feeding on the wet wooden, load-bearing components.

When mold is suspected of causing major material damage to the structural integrity of a building, a structural engineer or other professional with relevant expertise should be consulted.

Carpeting

Bathrooms and basements should not be carpeted. Carpeting installed on un-insulated concrete floors at ground level is of particular concern because of the potential for dampness, condensation and mold growth.

Check Other Areas for Mold Exposure

The following areas have a high potential for mold exposure:

- antique shops;
- greenhouses;
- saunas;
- barns;
- mills;
- construction areas;

- flower shops;

- summer cottages; and

- any area where grass is regularly mowed.

Measure Small, Medium or Large

The size and extent of the apparent mold problem should be measured. Mold contamination can generally be divided into small jobs (less than 10 square feet of mold), medium (10 to 100 square feet of mold), and large jobs (more than 100 square feet of mold). A remediation manager should be consulted for medium jobs. An experienced health and safety professional should be consulted for remediation projects and on large or complex jobs.

Use IAC2

Finding mold in buildings involves performing a non-invasive, visual examination and mold sampling, according to a standard. The IAC2 Mold Inspection Standards of Practice can be used as a guide to perform a mold inspection.

Use Computer Software

Finding mold in buildings requires documentation of work. A computer software program to document findings and write the inspection report can be utilized.

Quiz on Section 8

1. A(n)_____ inspection is the most important first step in identifying possible mold contamination.

    ☐ visual

    ☐ mold

    ☐ home

    ☐ invasive

    ☐ exhaustive

    ☐ micro-organism

2. T/F: The inspector shall report moisture intrusion, water damage, musty odors, apparent mold growth, or conditions conducive to mold growth.

    ☐ True

    ☐ False

3. T/F: Inspecting toilets is beyond the scope of a mold inspection.

    ☐ True

    ☐ False

4. Exposed dirt floors in _____ should be sealed with a vapor barrier.

    ☐ attic spaces

    ☐ detached garages

    ☐ carports

    ☐ bathrooms in basements

    ☐ under-floor crawlspaces

5. T/F: There is no reason to suspect mold if a building has a moldy smell but you don't see any mold.

    ☐ True

    ☐ False

6. T/F: Steam radiators are components whose operation is conducive to mold growth.

    ☐ True

    ☐ False

7. T/F: Excessive watering of house plants may create a condition conducive to mold growth.

    ☐ True

    ☐ False

8. T/F: A lawn sprinkler could create a condition conducive to mold growth.

☐ True
☐ False

9. T/F: It is possible to perform a professional and thorough mold inspection without a moisture meter.

☐ True
☐ False

10. T/F: A dryer vent that exhausts into the interior of the building is not within the scope of concern for a mold inspector.

☐ True
☐ False

11. T/F: An increase (up to 90%) in the relative humidity of air downstream of cooling coils is a natural result of the energy transfer between the air and the coils.

☐ True
☐ False

12. T/F: Mold needs some light to grow; it cannot grow in areas of complete darkness.

☐ True
☐ False

13. T/F: Micro-organisms can grow on the damp filter of an HVAC system, and even on the collected dust of its filter.

☐ True
☐ False

14. T/F: Poor or delayed maintenance of the HVAC system is a condition conducive to mold growth.

☐ True
☐ False

Answer Key is on page 150.

Section 9: Inspection Tools and PPE

Tools Necessary for a Mold Inspection

Eyes

The most important equipment to use during an examination for mold growth in a building includes your own eyes and nose. A visual examination of the building is required because sampling alone is almost useless.

Nose

Check for odors. Air sampling may be necessary if the presence of mold is suspected (as evidenced by musty odors), but the presence of mold cannot be confirmed by a visual examination. Musty and moldy odors are likely indications of mold growth.

Flashlight

A good flashlight is essential.

Moisture Meter

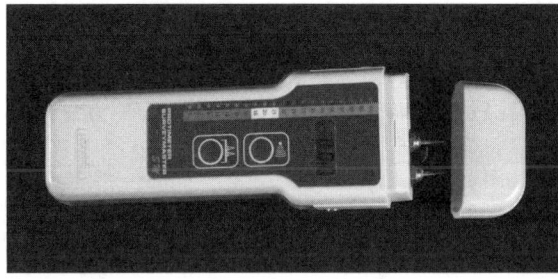

A mold inspector should use a moisture meter to find wet areas. Wherever there is moisture, dampness or wetness, there may be mold growing. Some areas having the greatest potential for microbial growth include groundwater intrusion, roof leaks, condensation, and plumbing leaks. Mold can grow instantly. It does not take 24 or 48 hours, or a few days to grow.

These meters measure the moisture in many types of building materials (substrates). They also can monitor the process of drying these materials. A moisture meter typically has a thin probe that can be inserted into the material to be tested, or pressed directly against its surface. Moisture meters can be used on carpet, wallboard, wood, brick and concrete. Because mold often grows where moisture is high, a moisture meter can help an inspector locate hidden areas of mold growth.

Digital Camera

A digital camera should be used to take pictures of all the sampled surfaces. A digital image should be taken of all of the areas of moisture intrusion, water-damaged components, areas of apparent mold growth, rooms with musty odors, and any other systems or components of the building that may be harboring mold growth.

IR Camera

An infrared camera can be used to detect moisture penetration that may not be visible to the human eye. An infrared camera is an inspection tool with many applications. It is a non-invasive instrument that can give clues to conditions that are behind the surface of a wall, floor and ceiling.

Humidity Gauge

An inspector should measure the humidity while performing an examination of the building. High humidity inside a building can lead to mold growth, so humidity gauges are very useful. When high humidity levels are measured inside a particular area or room in a building, that measurement may indicate hidden mold growth. Further evaluation is needed when high humidity levels are measured and mold growth is not visible.

There are measurement tools that measure both humidity and air temperature. The tool may have an infrared device for non-contact temperature measurements.

Borescope

Some investigators use borescopes to look for mold growth behind walls, without significantly damaging the drywall. A borescope may be useful when there is moisture intrusion, water damage, apparent mold growth, musty odors, or conditions conducive to mold growth, and the full extent of the problem cannot be ascertained by a visual inspection alone.

A borescope is often used when moisture penetration is apparent at a wall but the extent of the moisture problem is suspected to originate within the wall's cavity. Mold may be growing behind a finished wall or above a finished ceiling. With a borescope, an inspector can view the wall cavity without significant removal of or damage to the finished wall or ceiling. Written permission must be obtained from the property owner prior to using a borescope because one or more holes may need to be drilled through the finished wall or ceiling. The use of a borescope is beyond the IAC2 Standards of Practice.

Other Inspection Tools and Equipment:

- **duct tape:** for sealing the sleeves and legs of a work suit;

- **digital camera (with fresh batteries, and extra batteries):** for documenting inspection restrictions and conditions observable on the day of the inspection;

- **probe or poker;**

- **screwdriver and hand tools:** for probing or knocking. Decayed and damaged wood components produce sounds that are different from sounds produced by solid wood;

- **flashlight (with fresh batteries):** use rechargeable batteries, and carry extra batteries into the crawlspace and other dark areas;

- **laser pointer;**

- **headlight or headlamp (with extra batteries):** can be used as a backup to a flashlight, and can be used as the primary light source; headlamps keep your hands free;

- **non-contact voltage detector (with a beeper indicator):** to check electrical wires and their condition. Oftentimes, an inspector will discover loose, disconnected, live wires hanging from the crawlspace ceiling;

- **work lights:** have the advantage over flashlights by flooding the space with light, and a work light does not require the use of hands;

- **GFCI protection:** especially when using a work light with an extension cord. Many extension cords have integrated GFCI-protection devices;

- **extension cord:** with a heavy-gauge cable, at least 14-gauge (12-gauge wire is better). Make sure the cord is plugged into a properly wired and grounded receptacle;

- **carpet square:** for cleanliness. Use the carpet to stand upon after exiting a crawlspace or attic, particularly if the access is an interior opening and the space is muddy;

- **GFCI tester:** to test all electrical receptacles prior to using them;

- **measuring tape;**

- **moisture meter:** to confirm what is visually observed;

- **moisture gauge:** to confirm what is felt as musty, muggy or moisture-laden air;

- **infrared camera:** to discover moisture penetration that cannot be seen with the human eye. Use a quality holster or carrying bag to offer padded protection; and

- **a notepad and business cards:** When working in a vacant house, leave a note and a business card somewhere in the entry area to alert people entering the house of your location, and the reason for your presence.

Personal Protection Equipment (PPE)

We learned about inspection tools and equipment. Now let's go over PPE.

Mold inspectors are exposed to a variety of hazards, including insects, wildlife, construction debris, abrasions, dust, asbestos, lead, bio-aerosols, and mold spores. Since mold spores can enter the inspector's body through touch, ingestion and inhalation, PPE is very important. The primary function of PPE is to avoid inhaling mold and mold spores and to avoid coming into contact with mold through the skin and eyes. The use of PPE should be considered a requirement for mold inspectors. PPE protects against the hazards of working inside a mold-contaminated area of a building by limiting the inspector's exposure.

Personal and professional judgment should be used when selecting the appropriate PPE.

The Occupational Safety and Health Administration (OSHA) regulates the use of PPE in commercial and remediation work areas. OSHA requires the use of PPE for working in moldy environments, especially for remediation work. Anyone using respirators and other PPE in the workplace must be trained, must have a medical clearance, and must be fit-tested by a trained professional. Note that all OSHA regulations and requirements must be met.

To ensure a safe work environment for everyone performing inspections and remediation work, efforts to protect against exposure to mold contamination must be taken. Working in a mold-contaminated building can be hazardous. Good work practices and safety precautions must be followed to prevent or effectively mitigate mold exposure.

Hand Protection

There are many types of gloves available for inspections and remediation work. There are gloves that are chemical-resistant, cotton, canvas, puncture-resistant, disposable latex, and leather. Thick work gloves are best when bagging debris and materials. Rubber gloves can protect from electrical hazards. Leather gloves protect from abrasions and cuts. For mold inspections, disposable latex gloves are recommended, but not necessary. A mold sampling can be performed according to sampling protocols without wearing gloves.

Gloves protect the skin from contact with mold. They also protect the skin from potentially irritating cleaning solutions. Long gloves that extend to the middle of the forearm are recommended when disturbing mold. The material from which gloves are made should be suited to the type of materials being handled. When using a biocide in remediation work, such as chlorine bleach, or a strong cleaning solution, gloves should be made from natural rubber, neoprene, nitrile, polyurethane, or polyvinylchloride (PVC). If a mild detergent is being used, ordinary household rubber gloves are suitable. The routine use of biocides is not recommended.

Protective Clothing

Inspectors entering an under-floor crawlspace should wear protective clothing. Protective clothing is recommended for medium and large remediation projects. It prevents the transfer and spread of mold to clothing and eliminates skin contact with mold. When limited protection is warranted, disposable paper coveralls can be used. When full protection is required, a body suit of breathable material, such as Tyvek®, and mold-impervious disposable head and foot coverings should be used. All gaps, such as those around ankles and wrists, should be sealed. (Many remediators use duct tape to seal clothing.)

Foot Protection

Boots can provide protection from a variety of hazards and environmental and work conditions. For maximum protection, boots should have rubber soles. Shoe covers are needed to prevent the transfer of contamination to clean work areas or back home.

Eye Protection

Eye protection should be worn during an inspection where mold is visually evident. Airborne mold spores, particles and materials can enter the body through the eyes. Goggles, safety glasses and eye shields are readily available. Safety glasses or goggles that have open vent holes are not acceptable. A full-face respirator provides eye protection. A lower-face respirator does not. It is important to choose the proper type of eye protection, since most work-related eye injuries can't be prevented if using inadequate protection.

Head Protection

Any job that involves construction, demolition or building requires wearing a hard hat. Mold remediation work involves hazards that can be prevented by wearing head protection. Inspection work is no exception. There are different types of hard hats and head protection. There are hard hats, bump caps, face-shield adapters, and face-shield visors. Each type of head protection gear is designed for protection against specific hazards. Class A helmets are general-purpose. Class B helmets are for electrical work. Class C helmets are designed primarily for comfort; they are lightweight and offer limited protection. There is a label inside of each helmet showing the manufacturer's name, ANSI standard, and classification.

Respirators

The use of PPE is especially necessary when mold is disturbed and likely to become airborne during a surface sampling. It may be unavoidable to have mold spores released into the air during an inspection or remediation, and airborne spores can pose a health threat when they are inhaled. Allergic reactions to mold may manifest when mold spores enter through the respiratory system. Therefore, a respirator is commonly used. There are many different types of respirators. The choice of respirator depends upon the job's scope, contamination conditions, and the requirements of the work to be done. The respirator is an important piece of PPE.

Respirators protect inspectors and remediation workers from inhaling airborne mold, mold spores and dust. There are three classifications of respiratory protection that are generally used: minimum, limited and full. Only respirators approved by the National Institute for Occupational Safety and Health (NIOSH) should be worn during mold remediation. These respirators must be used according to applicable OSHA regulations.

Use minimum PPE when cleaning up a small area affected by mold (less than 10 square feet total). Minimum PPE includes gloves, goggles/eye protection, and an N-95 respirator. An N-95 respirator covers the nose and mouth, filters out 95% of airborne particulates, and is available at most hardware stores. However, it does not provide eye protection.

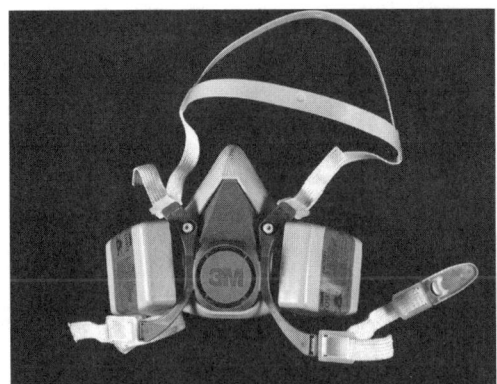

Limited PPE includes the use of half-face or full-face air-purifying respirators (APRs) equipped with P100 filter cartridges. These respirators have inhalation and exhalation valves that filter the air and ensure that it is free of mold particles. The P100 filters do not remove vapors or gases, and the half-face APRs do not protect the wearer's eyes. Limited PPE may be warranted when the total surface area affected by mold is between 10 and 100 square feet. Professional judgment should be used to make the final determination about whether to wear limited PPE.

Full PPE includes a full-face, powered air-purifying respirator (PAPR). It is recommended when more than 100 square feet of mold is found, when high levels of airborne dust or mold spores are likely, and/or when intense or long-term exposures are expected. A powered air-purifying respirator uses a blower to force air through a P100 filter. The filtered air is supplied to a mask that covers the wearer's face, or a hood that covers the entire head. Positive pressure within the hood prevents unfiltered air from entering through penetrations or gaps. Individuals must be trained to use their respirators before they begin remediation.

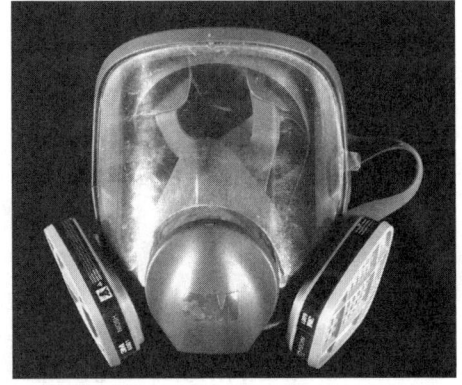

OSHA Regulations for Respirators

The human respiratory system can endure only a small amount of exposure to toxic gases, fumes and particles before becoming dangerously affected. Some inhaled chemicals will destroy portions of the lungs. Chemicals in the lungs can be absorbed into the bloodstream, affecting tissues and organs. Respirators can filter gases, vapors and particles in the air.

OSHA regulates the use of respirators in commercial workplaces. The agency states that all respirators must be approved and color-coded according to the known hazards, as well as individually fitted.

Respiratory protection should be used when the concentration of airborne substances exceeds the limit of specific exposure. There are several exposure limits that can be used to determine the type of respirator required for a given job. They include OSHA Permissible Exposure Limits, NIOSH Recommended Exposure Limits, and ACGIH Threshold Limit Values.

If none of these is used for mold inspection work, then other published data may be used, since there are no mold-spore exposure limits for inspectors defined by those three national groups and federal agencies. It is up to the mold inspector's discretion to determine when, where, and what type of respirator to use (if at all).

Some of OSHA's requirements for the minimum-acceptable standards for use of respirators in the workplace are:

- A written standard operating procedure governing respirators shall be available.

- Respirators are to be selected based upon the hazards to which the worker will be exposed.

- The worker shall be trained on how to use a respirator properly.

- Respirators shall be regularly cleaned, maintained and inspected.

- The work area shall be inspected to maintain good working conditions.

The selection of a proper respirator depends on:

- the nature of the hazards;

- the nature of the work or activity in the hazardous area;

- the location of the hazardous area in relation to a safe area having clean, breathable air;

- the length of time of exposure to hazards;

- the effectiveness of the respirator; and

- the individual fit of the respirator.

There are respirators that purify or filter the air. These have filters (for particulates), cartridges (for gases and vapors), or canisters (large-capacity gas masks). They require that the oxygen level be greater than 19.5%.

There are respirators that supply breathable air. They include a self-contained breathing apparatus, a supplied-air respirator, or a unit which is a combination of the two.

Filtering Disposable Face Mask

A particulate N-95 respirator is an air-purifying respirator used to provide protection in dusty, non-oil based environments, including jobs involving sanding, bagging and/or grinding. This respirator is lightweight in construction. It has a crimpable nose clip to provide a customized fit. This type is not recommended for mold inspectors.

Lower-Face or Half-Mask Respirator

A lower-face respirator has a face-sealing flange and chin holder. It has a head harness. The cartridges are disposable. The filters are job- and hazard-specific. The filters are readily available and easy to replace. It does not provide full protection.

Full-Face Respirator

The full-face respirator has dual cartridge attachments. A full field of vision is provided. It has a sealing flange and a head harness. It provides the greatest protection. This mask is best for mold remediation work and mold inspection work. A mold inspector working inside a crawlspace should wear a respirator.

In mold remediation of heavily contaminated areas, a powered air-purifying respirator or a supplied-air respirator may be needed for maximum protection. A self-contained breathing apparatus may be used, too.

Filters and Cartridges

Organic vapors produced by mold spores can be filtered. The cartridges for these are color-coded black for easy identification.

There are two classifications for respiratory hazards in relation to filters and cartridges. They are particulates and vapors/gases. Particulates can be filtered by mechanical means. Vapors and gases are filtered by absorbents that react chemically with them. To effectively remove both hazards, a respirator can combine both a mechanical filter and chemical sorbents.

There are three levels of filter effectiveness: a 95 rating is 95% effective, a 99 rating is 99% effective, and a 100 rating is 99.97% effective.

The service life of a filter or cartridge depends upon:

- sorbent quality;
- exposure conditions;
- relative humidity;
- temperature;
- concentration of the contaminant;
- type of gas or vapor; and
- the presence of other hazards or particulates.

OSHA requires testing the fit of all tight-fitting respirators on individuals. Fit-testing is required for the first-time use, and then annually afterwards. Each make, model and size of tight-fitting respirators should be fit-tested. The wearer may actually breathe contaminated air unless the air passes effectively through the filter or canister (or air-supply system). It is imperative that all respirators fit properly.

PPE by Classification:

- **minimum:** gloves, N-95 respirator, and goggles/eye protection;

- **limited:** gloves, N-95 respirator or half-face respirator with HEPA filter, disposable overalls, and goggles/eye protection;

- **full:** gloves, disposable full-body clothing, head gear, foot coverings, and full-face respirator with HEPA filter.

Basic PPE:

- **mask/respirator:** a full-face type should be used for remediation work. Lower-face or full-face can be used for inspections. Respirators are used to protect the lungs and eyes. Do not use a dust mask or paper mask as a substitute for a respirator;

- **work suit:** a full-body version with long sleeves will provide protection from hazards, including simple abrasions;

- **pockets:** to carry inspection tools while leaving your hands free;

- **knee pads:** to provide protection from rocks, water, debris, nails, concrete, etc.;

- **protective gloves (cloth or latex):** should not be so loose that it is difficult to operate a digital camera;

- **protective cloth cap:** or hard hat, if inspecting a potentially dangerous area;

- **work shoes:** worn only for working in moldy environments; and

- **shoe covers.**

Be Safe!

Safety is very important for all types of jobs, especially inspections and remediation work. Take the proper precautions to keep the work environment safe, train well in safety procedures, and wear PPE.

Section 10: Hypotheses

Topics Covered in This Section:

- Null Hypothesis

- "Damaged Building" Hypothesis

- "Aesthetic" Hypothesis

- "Affected Health" Hypothesis

- "That Which Is Visible Is Mold" Hypothesis

- Examples

All scientific disciplines share a similar approach to acquiring knowledge. The scientific method involves collecting data and observing evidence, and then drawing inferences from it. One school of thought holds that sampling can only disprove a hypothesis, and an inspector can never prove a cause-and-effect relationship. An alternative understanding of the basis of scientific knowledge is that all inspectors begin with a set of prior beliefs or assumptions. For example, an inspector may begin an examination of a building with an underlying assumption that there exist numerous undiscovered deficiencies in the building. Progress is made as hypotheses (based upon prior beliefs) are tested by the empirical evidence collected, which then either supports or refutes the hypotheses and underlying beliefs.

Before any sampling takes place, an inspector should develop a set of hypotheses that address the concerns of the client. A hypothesis is a proposition set forth as an explanation for the specific observation or condition experienced. A hypothesis is often used to guide the inspection (a "working" hypothesis) and can be accepted as highly probable in light of the established facts.

Hypotheses concerning the suspected role of fungal (mold) exposure on adverse conditions should be developed before any mold sampling takes place. The inspector and client should agree to the hypotheses and agree upon how they should be addressed.

The inspector needs to gather information, develop hypotheses, test the hypotheses, and make recommendations based upon all available information gathered.

Gather Information

Gathering information involves asking the client about their concerns about mold, the reasons why they are requesting a mold inspection, and what relevant information they expect to receive from an inspection. Setting expectations with the client is part of this information-gathering process.

There are generally three types of concerns clients may express about mold growth in a building:

1) the potential health effects of exposure to fungi and their byproducts;

2) the effect of mold contamination on the structural integrity of the building; and

3) the negative aesthetic effects fungi can produce both visually and on the human olfactory system.

Although the issue of whether exposure to indoor fungi causes adverse health effects is controversial, there is no doubt that a severely mold-contaminated building can suffer structural damage, and that a foul-smelling, fungus-filled building is aesthetically displeasing. Controversies about health effects aside, the latter two concerns are sufficient to merit a Complete Mold Inspection and remediation when an environment is found to have fungal contamination.

People who have concerns about structural damage or the aesthetic effects of indoor fungi should seek the services of a certified mold inspector. People who have concerns about the health effects of mold exposure should seek the advice of a healthcare professional.

There are generally eight questions that can be answered by a visual examination and mold sampling of a building:

   1) Is there water intrusion in the building?

   2) Are there any components in the building that are water-damaged?

   3) Are there musty, moldy odors in the building?

   4) Is there any visible, apparent mold?

   5) Is that which is visible actually mold?

   6) Are there indications of hidden mold growth?

   7) Are there conditions conducive to mold growth?

   8) What should be done if mold growth is discovered?

To address these concerns, hypotheses and questions appropriately, a visual examination must be performed to a standard, mold samples must be taken according to procedures, laboratory analysis must be included, and accurate reporting must be documented. Proper collection, handling and documentation of mold samples are all required for a conclusive, credible report. All inspection procedures should be followed carefully and precisely. Poor handling can lead to mistakes, errors, and exposure to liability.

Develop Hypotheses

There are generally four types of hypotheses about fungi in an indoor environment that can be developed by the inspector and the client:

   1) There is no mold growth in the building (the Null Hypothesis).

   2) The occupants' health is being affected by mold exposure (the "Health-Affected" Hypothesis).

   3) Structural damage has been caused by mold growth in the building (the "Damaged Building" Hypothesis).

   4) A musty odor indicates mold growth (the "Aesthetic" Hypothesis).

Null Hypothesis

An inspector should approach a mold inspection without bias toward finding mold. It is reasonable to assume that a building does not have a mold-growth problem. If the client does not have any concerns, then the inspector should assume that there are no mold growth problems in the building (null hypothesis). The inspector should approach the mold inspection without any presumption of a mold problem existing in the building. An assumption that there is no mold growth in the building should be made prior to performing a mold inspection. That way, if an actual mold problem is found at the building, it will be unexpected. Legally, it is a stronger argument that a mold inspector initiated a mold inspection without bias, without a presumption that a mold problem existed in a building. If your client does not express a particular concern about mold in the building, then make the null hypothesis and assume that there is no mold in the building prior to performing the inspection.

"Damaged Building" Hypothesis

If damage to the building is suspected to have been caused by fungal contamination, then a reasonable hypothesis would be that mold is present and is harming the building.

"Aesthetic" Hypothesis

Another hypothesis is that observable stains and odors are being caused by the presence of mold.

"Affected Health" Hypothesis

Health effects due to the exposure to indoor mold may depend on the types of mold present. Under certain circumstances, such as when litigation is involved, the source of the mold is uncertain, or health concerns are an issue, consider sampling as part of the site evaluation.

Concerns about health effects are more complicated because they involve a chain of hypotheses: mold has to be present; the affected person must be exposed to the mold; the affected person must be sensitive to such exposure; and the exposure must be the cause of the symptoms. Since that chain of hypotheses are very difficult (if not impossible) to prove during a mold inspection, then an inspector should apply the statements and conclusions made by credible sources (such as health professionals, the EPA, state health departments, indoor air quality associations, and others in the industry) who comment upon mold standards and guidelines in relation to health effects. Inspectors should make good use of this research as relevant, suitable and pertinent for interpreting laboratory results and making recommendations to their clients.

The purpose of a non-invasive, visual examination is to report moisture intrusion, water damage, apparent mold growth, musty odors, and conditions conducive to mold growth.

Determinations regarding a person's sensitivity to fungi, and the assessment of the relationship between that sensitivity and the person's symptoms, should be determined by healthcare professionals guided by the results of the mold sample taken by a mold inspector. It is not the inspector's responsibility to correlate mold in a building to their client's actual health.

"That Which Is Visible Is Mold" Hypothesis

According to the Environmental Protection Agency (EPA), "In most cases, if visible mold is present, sampling is unnecessary." An inspector may object to that statement because of the assumption that what is present is actually mold. There may be many inspectors who are comfortable in making that assumption.

"That which is visible is mold" is a statement based upon assumption. Apparent mold growth cannot be confirmed as actual mold growth by visual examination only.

The only way to know that what is visible is actually mold is through sampling. If neither the inspector nor the client has a need to confirm that what is seen is actually mold, then there is no need to sample. However, there may be other people affected by the findings of the inspector's report who will request proof or validation of such visual findings.

The term "visible mold" applies to what appears only on the surface, and not to what is borne out by professional examination, scientific sampling, and confirmation by laboratory analysis. The term "visible mold" should not be used in reference to actual mold growth. The term "visible, apparent mold" is accurate.

Not everything that looks like mold is mold. Paint on the backside of drywall or wood may look like mold growth. Alkaline crystals on soil or concrete walls may look like mold, but, unlike mold, they are usually water-soluble. Carpet stains also may look like mold. Spider webs, fine dust, dried paint spray, dried mud, and water stains may all give the appearance of mold growth. The inspector who reports the existence of mold growth based upon the discovery of something that merely appears to look moldy may be in error. It may be mold; it may not. Error comes with guessing.

A rule of thumb is: Don't guess. It is considered an inspector's due diligence to act and perform with care, and to report with accuracy. A professional inspector should report "the presence of visible mold" based upon fact and evidence, and avoid making possibly inaccurate assumptions about mere surface appearances.

Most microbiology laboratories need only a little of the suspected mold on a clear strip of sticky tape to determine, using a microscope, whether it is actually mold or just something that looks like mold. Sampling may help locate the source of the mold contamination, identify some of the mold species present, and differentiate between mold and soot or dirt.

Test Hypotheses

Test the hypotheses by collecting and analyzing all relevant information about the building and its systems and components, by performing a non-intrusive, visual examination, and by taking multiple mold samples. The mold sampling should be in alignment with the client's concerns about the suspected mold. In an attempt to conserve time, money and resources, the amount, type and location of samples should directly address the hypotheses that have been developed by the inspector and the client.

Make Recommendations

After finding apparent mold growth, the goal is to confirm that it is, in fact, mold. Reporting mold growth with care and accuracy is accomplished through sampling by a certified inspector and analysis by a laboratory. Sampling should be conducted if mold is suspected. After confirming mold growth at high or elevated concentration levels inside the building, then cleaning up and/or removal of the mold growth and contaminated building materials should be recommended. There are several sources to refer to when making mold remediation recommendations.

An Example of a Hypothesis

The following is an example of a hypothesis an inspector can use as a guide.

After speaking with the client, the inspector first asserts a null hypothesis, stating, "There is no mold growth at the building that could affect the health of the occupants, cause structural damage, or produce odors. And there are no conditions conducive to mold growth."

While performing a non-invasive, visual examination of the building, the inspector then finds visible, apparent mold growth on the drywall of a non-load-bearing wall in the basement near the hot water source.

Additional assumptions (hypotheses) are made by the inspector:

1) The apparent mold growth is, in fact, actual mold growth.

2) Enough moisture exists in this area of the building to support mold growth.

3) Mold spores from this growth area are floating in the air (the breathing zone) of the rooms in which the building's occupants dwell.

4) The mold may affect the health of those exposed.

The inspector determines that further evaluation is needed in order to find the source of moisture in the building that is supporting the apparent mold growth. The use of a moisture meter or other device can provide an objective indication of the amount of moisture in a building's material. A closer examination of the area by the inspector, using a moisture meter, results in the discovery of significant moisture coming from a dripping temperature and pressure-relief valve on the hot water tank. The wall material is discovered to be wicking moisture up from the floor where the water drip is located.

The inspector determines that a surface sampling is needed to confirm the existence of actual mold growth. The inspector determines that air sampling is also needed to address the concern that mold spores may affect the health of those exposed.

A surface mold sampling of the area of apparent mold growth is taken. The result of the surface mold sampling confirms that the visible apparent mold is, in fact, actual microbial growth (mold). Ultimately, the presence of microbial growth, which is only possible if water is available, provides evidence that sufficient moisture is present to aid the mold growth.

Multiple air samples are taken. (The biological agents of interest are fungal allergens, but detection of fungal spores is often used to indicate allergen presence.) The results of the air sampling confirm that there are elevated levels of mold spores in the air of the basement, as compared with the control samples taken outside the building.

The initial null hypothesis that there is no mold growth at the building that could affect the occupants' health, cause structural damage, or produce odors, and that there are no conditions conducive to mold growth, was disproved and found to be false. The evidence outlined in support of the three assumptions or additional hypotheses (that the apparent mold growth is, in fact, actual mold growth; enough moisture exists to support mold growth; and mold spores are floating in the air) are sufficient to conclude that the source of excessive moisture in the basement should be addressed, and the water-damaged (mold-contaminated) wall material should be replaced.

The fourth assumption about health should not be directly commented upon by the mold inspector.

Since there was, in fact, moisture intrusion and mold growth in the building, and since there was an elevated concentration of mold spores measured in the air, the potential for negative health effects caused by mold exposure exists. As a result, the inspector should make a recommendation that the client consult a healthcare professional with regard to exposure to the mold and any subsequent negative health effects. Information about negative health effects related to mold exposure, as well as recommendations to remediate the mold problem in the building, should be provided to the client in the mold inspection report.

Another Example of a Hypothesis

An inspector makes the hypothesis that there is not a mold growth problem inside the HVAC ductwork system (a null hypothesis).

Air samples are taken before and after the HVAC system is turned on. Air samples show a significantly lower concentration of mold spores in the air before the HVAC system was turned on than after it was turned on and operated for 15 minutes.

The sampling results may be convincing that there is a mold growth problem inside the ductwork, and mold spores are being circulated throughout the building when the HVAC system is turned on.

Quiz on Section 10

1. Before taking any samples, an inspector should develop a set of _____ that address the concerns of the client.

     ☐ numbers

     ☐ facts

     ☐ mold tests

     ☐ conclusions

     ☐ answers

     ☐ hypotheses

2. "Stains and odors are caused by the presence of mold" is an example of a(n) _____ hypothesis.

     ☐ mycotoxic

     ☐ aesthetic

     ☐ esoteric

     ☐ presence

     ☐ confirmation

3. T/F: Not everything that looks like mold is mold.

     ☐ True

     ☐ False

4. T/F: The mold sampling should be in alignment with the client's concerns about mold.

     ☐ True

     ☐ False

Answer Key is on page 151.

Section 11: Sampling Devices

Bio-Aerosol Impaction Sampler

A single-stage bio-aerosol impaction sampler is an aluminum device held together by three spring clamps and sealed with O-ring gaskets.

The impactor's stage contains 400 precision-drilled holes. When air is drawn through the sampler, multiple jets of air on the stage direct any airborne particles toward a collection surface coated with agar. To ensure the sample's integrity, the sampling device, such as the EMS E6, must be used with a pump capable of handling 28.3 liters per minute.

Reuter Centrifugal Sampler

With centrifugal samplers, the principle behind the device's collection is centrifugation. It involves the creation of a vortex in which particles with sufficient inertia leave the airstream to impact upon a collection surface, such as a semi-solid medium of agar. After the sampling is finished, the agar strip is then sent to a laboratory for analysis. The most common type of this device is the Reuter Centrifugal Air Sampler.

Airborne Particle Counters

Airborne particle counters (APCs) are hand-held, battery-operated instruments that also measure temperature and relative humidity. An APC has four parts: the sensor; the pump; the battery; and its electronics. The pump draws about 0.1 cubic feet of air per minute.

This device produces a sample that requires laboratory analysis. It identifies only the size of the particles that are airborne. The APC measures two particle size ranges simultaneously: 0.5 and 5 microns. Some measure four size ranges of particles simultaneously, including: 0.3, 0.5, 1 and 5 microns. Some APCs have three sampling modes and can display data in particles per cubic foot, particles per liter, and total particles. The sample count and sample interval times can be user-programmed. The date, time and particle counts for up to 200 locations are stored in the device's memory for later on-screen review and for downloading to a printer or personal computer.

Air-O-Cell®

The Air-O-Cell® is a unique air sampling cassette designed specifically for the rapid collection of a wide range of airborne aerosols, including mold spores, pollen, insect parts, skin cell fragments, fibers (such as asbestos, fiberglass, cellulose, clothing fibers, etc.), and inorganic particulates (such as ceramic, fly ash, copier toner, etc.). The Air-O-Cell® collects both viable and non-viable sample specimens, providing a much broader overview of potential allergens and contaminants than conventional sampling techniques and devices.

The Air-O-Cell® operates on the principle of inertial impaction. Particulate-laden air is accelerated as it is drawn through the cassette's tapered inlet slit, and directed toward a small slide containing the collection media, where the particles become impacted, and the air flow continues out the exit orifice. The adhesive nature of the collection media prevents the collected particulate from blurring or being washed off during the laboratory staining process, and also eliminates loss of the sample due to vibration during handling and shipment.

After sampling is completed, the cassettes are sent to a laboratory where the slides are removed, and direct microscopic analysis can be immediately performed. The collection media is compatible with a wide range of biological stains and refractive index oils, allowing direct, quantitative analysis of organic and inorganic particulates.

The Air-O-Cell® can be used with any standard off-the-shelf sampling pump capable of drawing 15 LPM in open flow. The compact size makes the Air-O-Cell® suitable for use in confined and restricted spaces.

BioCassette™

The BioCassette™ is similar to the Air-O-Cell® with regard to the pump and tubing. The difference between the two is that the BioCassette™ uses an agar base surface to collect the sample and allow it to grow. Anything that touches or comes in contact with the agar plate will contaminate the sample, and a new sample will be required.

Z5 Sampling Cassette

The "5-liter by five-minute" air-sampling cassette is made by Zefon. The Z5 sampling cassette is a cost-effective, first-line mold-screening tool that efficiently and reliably collects mold. It can be used by home inspectors to collect preliminary information on whether a mold problem may exist and further investigation is warranted.

The Z5 is a spore-trap impactor that uses slit impaction as the collection mechanism. This method is an industry-recognized and reliable method that allows easy mold-spore collection. It works with any pump set at a flow of 5 LPM.

The Z5 standard operating procedures are: 1) remove the caps from both ends of the Z5; 2) attach the vinyl tubing from the pump to the bottom of the Z5 (where the round cap was inserted); 3) turn pump on; 4) calibrate the pump before each use, making sure that the bottom of the stainless steel ball in the flow meter is sitting above the 5-liter line marker; 5) listen for suction; and 7) run pump for five minutes.

AC/DC IAQ (Indoor Air Quality) Pump

This pump is designed for mold inspectors who do not want to carry around extension cords. This pump runs on AC/DC power, providing the versatility to sample anywhere. It has a quick, two-hour fully-charged time. This pump can run for up to three hours of performance between charges. It has a built-in rotameter, a quick-release tubing attachment, a built-in digital countdown timer, and a rechargeable 12-volt battery. It can be charged when operating in AC mode. It has a HEPA filter exhaust system. It weighs about 15 pounds.

BUCK Libra Plus™ LP-7

This pump range is between 3 and 7 LPM to allow applications of the Micro 5 MicroCell spore-trap impactor cassette. A special five-minute timer in the main menu allows for a rapid start-up for samplers. Additional applications of the Libra Plus™ air sampling pump include drawing air contaminants in through a sampling media, such as 25 and 37 mm filter cassettes, to gauge personnel exposure to gases, vapors, particulates, aerosols, etc.

The sampler consists of a pump contained in a Lexan case, an exclusive and proprietary electronic circuit board for flow control, an LCD display with two lines of 16 characters, a single diaphragm pump mechanism, and a rechargeable nickel-metal hydride battery pack. Other features of the Libra Plus™ include displays for elapsed time, flow rate, and accumulated volume. The built-in timer counts down the sampling time and automatically turns off the pump. All data is saved and cleared for the next sample.

MegaLite Air Pump

The components include an air pump with a rotameter, a heavy-duty case, and a built-in flow control valve. It operates at a flow range of 3 to 30 LPM, and comes with 10 feet of vinyl tubing and a HEPA filter.

Rotary Vane Pump

This lightweight, low-maintenance, rotary vane sampler is specifically designed to be used for not only asbestos and spore-trap cassettes, but will work with impactors (with an adjustable flow range of 3 to 30 LPM). It comes complete with 6 feet of vinyl tubing, inline filters, muffler jar, feet, handle and built-in switch. It weighs 9.9 pounds.

Zefon Bio-Pump®

The Zefon Bio-Pump® is a portable, battery-powered pump that provides a simple and convenient way to sample with Air-O-Cell® cassettes at a flow rate of 15 LPM. It is portable and battery-powered. Its programmable timer allows unattended operation. It comes with a quick-charge battery charger.

Wall Sampling Attachment

The Air-O-Cell® inner wall sampler provides these features in a simple tubing attachment that works in conjunction with Air-O-Cell® cassettes.

BioSIS™ Slide with Mailer

Individually packaged BioSIS™ Slides come with slide mailers, to be used for Allergenco-D and BioSIS™ samplers, which eliminate the possibility of cross-contamination.

Bio-Tape™

Bio-Tape™ provides a sampling method used for the determination of possible microbial, bio-aerosol, and inorganic dust contamination in a simple, standardized way. It provides the ability to quickly take a sample and measure the relative degree of contamination. It is especially useful when sampling valuable or non-transportable materials, and is very effective on smooth areas of concern.

Carpet Cassettes

Carpet cassettes are designed for the collection of fibers and particulates from carpets and other dusty areas. Carpet testing will give historical data of previous mold contamination. The cassettes use a 1-inch piece of tubing with a 45-degree bevel fitted to the inlet port, and come preloaded with 0.45μ and 5.0μ MCE filter, and support pad carpet sampling cassette. The chain-of-custody form and lab fee are included.

Culture Swabs

Culture swabs are easy to use for visual surface sampling. Convenient containers are included, which can be used for storage and transport.

Section 12: Air Sampling

Topics Covered in This Section:

- When to Take Air Samples

- Comparisons: Similar Times and Conditions

- Closed-Building Conditions

- HVAC Systems

- Air-Sampling Locations

- Outdoor Air Sampling: Weather Conditions and Air Flow

- Sampling Results: Limits of the Sampling

Inspectors collect air samples in order to test hypotheses about indoor environments. Air samples can detect and quantify the presence of mold spores, identify the release of mold spores into the air from mold-growth sources, aid in assessing human exposure to the mold spores, and monitor the effectiveness of control measures and remediation.

A primary way of testing for mold growth (or collecting bio-particulates) and answering concerns addressed by hypotheses is by air sampling.

If it is suspected that mold is present and harming the building, it is necessary to assume that spores or fungal byproducts have traveled from the sources of mold growth to living spaces and other areas of the building. The most direct way to identify paths through which spores move is to measure their concentration in the air along air-flow pathways. Air sampling can identify potentially damaging mold, even when mold growth is not readily visible.

An inspector may be able to establish that a plausible or demonstrable "exposure pathway" exists by taking and interpreting multiple air samples.

Air samples are taken by the use of a pump that pulls air through a collection device. The device catches mold spores from the air. The sample is sent to a laboratory, and a microscope is used to count the mold spores.

When to Take Air Samples

Consult the IAC2 Mold Sampling Procedures, the IAC2 Mold Inspection Standards of Practice, and the IAC2 Mold Sampling Decision Chart to assist in deciding when and where to take samples in a building.

In general, take air samples when a non-invasive, visual examination of the building reveals:

- moisture intrusion;

- water damage;

- musty odors;

- apparent mold growth; and/or

- conditions conducive to mold growth.

When such conditions exist, at least one interior air sample shall be taken by the mold inspector.

Two Outdoor Samples

In general, an inspector shall take two outdoor air samples of the highest-quality general air to be used as control samples (or background samples). If possible, one sample should be located on the windward-side of the building (the side facing the point from which the wind blows), and the other should be located on the leeward-side of the building (the side sheltered from the wind).

The outdoor sampling should begin soon after arriving at the property, assuming that the weather is clear and calm. It is better to perform the outdoor sampling while the weather is favorable than to wait. The outdoor conditions may change drastically during the examination and sampling of the building's interior.

The sampling device located on the windward-side of the building should be positioned so as to face the wind directly. The sampling device should point toward the wind, in the direction of the point from which the wind is blowing. The sampling device should be 3 to 6 feet from the ground surface (the breathable space). Typically, the device should be about 10 feet away from the front entry door. The idea is to have both outdoor samples located in areas where the device will collect a representative sampling of the air that may enter the building through the entry door or nearby open windows (the openings on the sides of the building).

If there is a main ventilation component of the building that draws fresh air into the building from the outside, the sampling should be performed 10 feet from that intake. The sampling should be performed at least 10 feet from the entrance to the home most frequently used. The sampling should not be performed under an overhang, soffit or eave, or carport, porch roof, or any other roof or overhead structure. The air sampling devices should be kept at least 10 feet away from all openings, air intakes, registers, exhaust vents, vent pipes, ventilation fans, etc.

HVAC Systems

Air sampling at the HVAC system may be necessary if there is suspicion based on a visual examination that the ventilation system may be contaminated, such as apparent mold growth on the coils, central humidifier, filter or supply registers. The purpose of such air sampling is to assess the extent of apparent contamination throughout the building. It is preferable to conduct sampling before and during the operation of the HVAC system.

At least one air sample shall be taken at an air supply register. Ideally, there would be at least three samples similarly situated, but financial or time constraints may limit the number of samples that can be taken. The air sample should be taken near an air supply register, with the sampling device oriented so that air from the register directly enters the sampling device. A gentle or vigorous mechanical agitation of the ductwork (a bump or shake) is appropriate.

Comparisons: Similar Times and Conditions

An air sample should be taken when apparent mold growth is visible. An air sample can be taken for other reasons, including evidence of moisture intrusion, water damage, a musty odor, or conditions conducive to mold growth. Samples of the indoor and outdoor air should be taken for comparison.

Note:

- There should not be any mold inside the house that is not found outside.

- The concentration of mold inside a home should not be higher than the concentration of mold outside.

Keep in mind that mold spores in the air being sampled can vary greatly in relation to the life cycle of the mold, atmospheric and environmental conditions, and the amount of ventilation. There are seasonal and diurnal variables in airborne mold at an indoor residential environment.

Air sampling may be necessary if the presence of mold is suspected (for example, as evidenced by musty odors), but cannot be identified by a visual examination alone. The purpose of such air sampling is to determine the location and/or extent of mold contamination. All mold spores have a source, and identifying the source is the goal.

Because the outdoor sample is the control sample, and it is used to compare with the indoor sample, the samples should be collected as close as possible in time and under similar conditions. Air samples should be collected at the same air-flow rate, for the same duration of time, near the same height above the floor in all rooms that are sampled indoors, and using the same type of collection device.

Closed-Building Conditions

Air sampling should be made under closed-building conditions. Closed-building conditions are necessary in order to stabilize the air that may contain mold spores or mVOCs, and to increase the reproducibility of the air sampling and measurement.

Windows (on all levels) and external doors should be kept closed (except during normal entry and exit) during the sampling period. Normal entry and exit include a brief opening and closing of a door but, to the extent possible, external doors should not be left open for more than a few minutes.

In addition, external-internal air-exchange systems (other than a furnace), such as high-volume, whole-house and window fans, should not be operating. However, attic fans intended to control attic temperature (and not whole-building temperature or humidity) should continue to operate. Combustion or make-up air supplies must not be closed.

Normal operation of permanently installed energy-recovery ventilators (also known as heat-recovery ventilators or air-to-air heat exchangers) may also continue during closed-building conditions. In houses where permanent radon-mitigation systems have been installed, these systems should be functioning during the air-sampling period.

Closed-building conditions will generally exist as normal living conditions in northern areas of the country when the average daily temperature is low enough so that windows are kept closed. Depending on the geographical area, this can be the period from late fall to early spring.

Air sampling should not be conducted during unusually severe storms or periods of unusually high winds. Severe weather will affect the sampling and analysis results in several ways. First, a high wind will increase the variability of airborne mold-spore concentration because of wind-induced differences in air pressure between the building's interior and exterior. Second, rapid changes in barometric pressure increase the chance of a large difference in the interior and exterior air pressures, consequently changing the rate of airborne mold spores being sucked into the building. Weather predictions available on local news stations can provide sufficient information to determine if these conditions are likely.

Air-Sampling Locations

Indoor air sampling should be performed near the center of each room or area of the building that has moisture intrusion, water damage, apparent mold growth, musty odors, or conditions conducive to mold growth.

If there are no areas of concern, then one air sampling should be made near the HVAC return (if that is available). Otherwise, at least one indoor air sample should be taken in the most lived-in common room, such as the family room or living room. More than one indoor air sample can be taken at the discretion of the inspector.

An indoor air sampling should take place only in the livable space in the building. Sampling in areas such as closets, under-floor crawlspaces, unfinished attics, storage or utility rooms, or inside the HVAC system is prohibited. The air collection device should be about 3 to 6 feet above the floor's surface.

Inside the building, the air-pump sampling should run for 10 minutes. If there is a lot of indoor activity, then the air-pump sampling should be reduced to five minutes. If there is an active source of dust, such as construction or cleaning, then the air-sampling time should be reduced to one minute.

Outdoor Air Sampling: Weather Conditions and Air Flow

On a chain-of-custody form, the weather conditions shall be recorded. The weather conditions should be clear and calm. High winds may affect the quality of the sample, including the comparison between indoor and outdoor samples.

On a clear, windless day, air-pump sampling should run for 10 minutes. When the outdoor air is something other than clear and windless, then the time of the sampling should be reduced to five minutes or less. A breeze, the mowing of grass, nearby construction, and dusty air can all affect the sampling conditions.

Air-pump sampling should not take place outdoors if it is raining. If possible, wait for at least two hours after the rain has stopped before taking an air-pump sample. Alterations or adjustments to the normal procedure or locations of taking air pump samples, particularly for the control sample, must be recorded in a chain-of-custody report.

Air pump sampling should not take place when the outdoor air temperature is below 32° F. All air sampling should take place when the air temperature is above freezing. If the ground is completely covered with snow, outdoor air-pump sampling should not be performed. A partial covering or a light dusting of snow is acceptable.

Air-Flow Rate

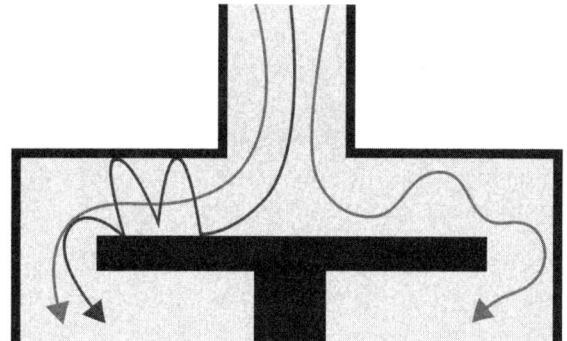

There are many different types of air pumps, measurement meters and spore collectors that can be used for air sampling at a mold inspection. The air pump should be adjusted to collect air at a flow rate that is recommended by the manufacturer. The result of an air pump sample is recorded in spores per meter, cubed (spores/m³). If the air-flow rate is too fast, the spores will bounce off the collector plate or slide and will not stick. If the air-flow rate is too slow, the spores float around the collector plate or slide and will not stick.

Rotameters are air-flow meters that provide field accuracy in an easy-to-read instrument. The principle of operation is simple: air flow passes through a vertical, tapered tube and pushes a small ball or float whose diameter is slightly less than the smaller end of the tube. As the little ball rises, the clearance between the ball and the tube wall increases. The ball becomes stationary when the diameter of the tube is large enough to allow the total air flow past the ball. The flow rate is determined by the number on the tube at the middle position of the stabilized ball.

Rotameter Tube

Air Flow

Sampling Results: Limits of the Sampling

Keep in mind that sampling provides information about a building as it existed at the time it was inspected. The results may not represent conditions at a time in the past or future. Changes in the types, concentrations and proportions of mold spores in the air can be rapid and substantial.

Section 13: Procedures for Air Sampling

1) The **sampling equipment** must be protected, clean and properly maintained at all times. The sampling devices shall be clean and free from dirt and debris prior to starting a sample. If re-usable collection devices are used, then they shall be handled and cleaned prior to use, in accordance with the manufacturer's recommendations. The re-usable collection device may need to be cleaned with an alcohol swab prior to use. The collector may have sticky slides already prepared, or the collector may utilize a one-time-use, self-contained device.

2) Slides, cassettes and **one-time-use devices** should be stored in cool and dry environments. The slides must be protected from direct sunlight. Sampling devices (slides, swabs, cassettes, tapes) older than one year should not be used.

3) Set the **air collector** at a normal breathing height, which is about 3 to 6 feet above the ground level or floor surface. A tripod is typically used to set the collector's height. The outdoor control sample should be taken at the same height as the indoor sample.

4) **Calibrate the flow of the pump.** Do not attach the sampling device (cassette) on the tubing yet. Measure the flow rate of the pump with a rotameter that has been calibrated to a standard. Make sure that the flow rate is set to the manufacturer's recommendations. For example, an Air-O-Cell® cassette's flow rate is 15 liters of air per minute. The pump should be calibrated regularly (once a day). A record of calibrations should be kept in a log book.

5) **After calibration,** securely attach the tubing of the pump to the sampling device (cassette). Turn on the pump. Start sampling. Record the start time.

6) **After turning on the air pump,** check the air-flow rate. The flow rate should not vary. A flow change greater than 5% requires a new air sample to be taken. All air samples must have the same volume.

7) A **digital time controller** on the equipment is highly recommended. Examine the collector. There should not be an overload on the slide. There should be a fine trace (hardly visible to the human eye) of dust and spores on the slide. A slide that has a visible trace on it may be unreadable. If that is the case, the environmental conditions may need improvement, or a new sampling location may be needed. If a slide is heavy, a new sample should be taken.

8) Remember, **all air samples** must have the same volume.

9) **Record the time** that the pump stopped. Mark the sampling device with a unique sampling number. Record that information on the chain-of-custody form.

10) Place slides in a protective carrying case, or close the collector, if a cassette is used. This protects the slides. **Prevent cross-contamination.** A new sample must be taken if a slide is accidentally touched, smeared or contaminated because it will be unreadable.

11) **Calculate the volume** by multiplying the liters of air pumped by the number of minutes. An example of the calculation is 20 liters of air pumped multiplied by 10 minutes equals 20 liters per minute or 200 liters (20L x 10 minutes = 200 L).

Section 14: Procedures for Surface Sampling

Surface sampling can provide information regarding whether the visible, apparent mold is, in fact, actual microbial growth (mold) or not. It can also measure the relative degree of the mold contamination, and it can serve to confirm that the sampled mold growth may be producing mold spores in the air.

Surface sampling is not destructive to building materials or surfaces when performed properly. For example, it may be possible to collect samples of fungal growth from the surfaces of valuable furnishings or materials of historical provenance or interest without damaging the original items.

Loose particles can be collected by pressing a contact plate to a surface, or by applying an adhesive material to lift off the visible, apparent mold growth.

Because there is direct contact with and disturbance of the mold-contaminated area involved in this type of testing, PPE is recommended, including gloves and a respirator rated at N-95 or higher.

Use the IAC2 Mold Sampling Decision Chart to assist in deciding when and where to take samples in a building.

Swab Sampling

A swab comes inside a plastic tube container. The cellulose swab is moistened with a liquid preservative stored in an ampoule at one end of the tube container. Any bacteria collected with the swab are transferred via the swab into a tube. The tube is sent directly to a laboratory for analysis.

A swab provides immediate determination of the presence of fungal spores, as well as what types of fungi are present.

Take swab samples when a non-invasive, visual examination of the building reveals:

- moisture intrusion;
- water damage;
- apparent mold growth;
- musty odors; and/or
- conditions conducive to mold growth.

A swab sample should be taken when apparent mold growth is visible. A swab sample can be taken for other reasons, including moisture intrusion, water damage, a musty odor, or conditions conducive to mold growth.

Benefits

There are benefits to using a swab sample. The swab sampling is inexpensive. It can be performed quickly. The swab sampling of a surface indicates all molds present in that particular sampled area. The swab sampling may reveal indoor reservoirs of spores that have not yet become airborne.

There are many manufacturers of swab sampling systems. Different manufacturers may have different methods for taking a sample with their particular swab system. Hold the tube container so that the ampoule with the liquid preservative is at the top. Pinch the plastic tube so the liquid will flow down onto the swab. To remove the moistened swab, pull on the cap. Rub and roll the wet swab over a 1-inch-square area of the apparent mold growth. The swab should collect visible, apparent mold. Insert the swab back into the tube. Secure the cap.

Each Sample

A unique sample number should be recorded for each swab sample. Write the number on the tube itself. The chain-of-custody document should include the sample number, location, date and time of the sampling.

Each Room

Take a sample in each room or area where there is visible, apparent mold.

Each Color

If there is apparent mold growth of different colors in the room or area, take a sample of each different-colored mold. The different colors may indicate different types of mold.

Each Substrate

If mold is visible on different substrates or building materials, such as wood, drywall or wallpaper, then taking a sample from each different material is recommended.

Tape Sampling

A tape system provides a quick way to sample visible mold. A tape-lift system is the most common surface-sampling technique. It can be used instead of a swab sample. Many samples can be collected in a short period of time. Samples that show hyphae fragments and reproductive structures can provide proof of mold growth.

There are many advantages of using tape-lift systems instead of regular tape. One of the most popular tape sampling products is Bio-Tape™. The Bio-Tape™ system is easier to handle, the tapes are individually numbered, it requires less laboratory preparation time, and the slides are flexible and will not break.

The sampling result is not quantitative. The presence of fungi can be confirmed, genera can be identified, and possibly a semi-quantitative estimation of the amount of each genus can be determined.

How to use a tape-lift system:

1) Remove the slide from the mailer.

2) Record the sample number and all other identification information prior to taking the sample.

3) Peel off the protective liner from the slide to expose the adhesive.

4) Place the slide with the sticky side down on the contaminated area being sampled.

5) Press down gently and make contact. Excessive pressure is not necessary.

6) Lift the slide from the surface and place it back into the mailer. Do not replace the protective liner.

7) Record all information on the chain-of-custody document, including the property's address, date, time, and sample number.

8) Mail the sample to the laboratory.

PPE

Because this type of sampling requires direct contact with and disturbance of the contaminated area, PPE is recommended, including gloves and a respirator rated at N-95 or higher.

Each Sample

A unique sample number should be recorded for each tape sample. The chain-of-custody document should include the sample number, location, date and time of the tape sampling.

Each Room

Take the tape sample in each room or area where there is visible, apparent mold.

Each Color

If there is apparent mold growth of different colors in the room or area, take a tape sample of each different-colored mold. The different colors may indicate different types of mold.

Each Substrate

If mold is visible on different substrates or building materials, such as wood, drywall or wallpaper, then taking a tape sample from each different material is recommended.

Carpet Sampling

Carpeting tends to contain the history of any mold that has been growing in the building. The carpet sampling is performed to reveal previous mold problems. A carpet sampling can also reveal undetected mold growth that may have been covered over or cleaned up. Choose an area that is not heavily walked upon—an area with little foot traffic. Do not sample under furniture.

An air pump and a carpet-sampling cartridge are used to vacuum a small area of the carpet. The cartridge should be inserted as deep as possible into the pile of the carpet. If the carpet has not been cleaned thoroughly prior to a sampling, it can easily hold evidence of a mold problem in the house. Even after cleaning, there can be mold spores discovered deep in the carpet.

Set up the air pump, a rotameter, and a carpet cartridge connected with tubing. The air flow of the pump should be set to 15 liters per minute. Sample an area equal to 4 inches by 4 inches. Sample a clean area of the carpet. If visible dirt collects on the filter, a new sample must be taken. Take a sample until a visible trace appears on the filter in the cartridge, but not for more than 10 minutes.

Bulk Sampling

Bulk or surface samples may need to be collected to identify specific fungal contaminants as part of a medical examination if occupants are experiencing symptoms that may be related to fungal exposure. This type of sampling may also be used to identify the presence or absence of mold if a visual inspection is inconclusive (if mold can be confused for discoloration or staining, for example).

Small pieces of carpet, drywall, or other porous building materials may be collected and mailed to a laboratory for analysis. It is unusual for an inspector to have permission to remove pieces of building material. Normally, a swab sample is taken instead of a bulk sample. Use a respirator and gloves when handling moldy bulk material. Mail to the laboratory only small pieces of material in airtight plastic bags. Double-bag the sample for safety during shipping and handling. The bag should be marked with unique sample numbers. Document the information on the chain-of-custody form.

mVOC Canister Sampling

A canister-based method has been developed for detecting microbial volatile organic compounds (mVOCs) in air. MVOCs have been determined to be an indicator of mold growth because their presence is associated with actively growing mold. Sampling for mVOCs can be used to detect hidden sources of mold. MVOCs have been sampled using sorbent tubes, but limited sample flow rates require the tube samples to be collected over one hour or longer. Canisters can be filled in just a few seconds, providing a faster means of screening an indoor environment for mold.

Data correlating the concentration of mVOCs to hazardous mold levels have been shown that below 8 ug/L of total mVOCs, most people will not have any allergic reaction; between 8 and 30 ug/L, some people may have moderate allergic reactions; and at levels above 30 ug/L, there will very likely be allergic reactions.

Wall Sampling

If a mold problem within a wall of a building is suspected, then a wall sampling can be performed. Written permission from the property owner must be obtained prior to sampling, since this is a destructive procedure. Wall sampling is beyond the IAC2 Standards of Practice.

A collector device is used to sample the air within the wall's interior or the wall cavity's air.

The sampling is performed by collecting air within a wall cavity (a non-livable space) and, therefore, the sample should not be used to compare to a control sample or to other samples. The air pump may collect a large amount of air that is equivalent to other samples, but it may be actually pulling air from other places, in addition to the wall cavity.

The sample of the wall's interior can be taken by inserting a tube in a small hole or gap near an electrical receptacle or where a wall switch is located. There is sometimes a gap or open space visible around the box after the cover plate is removed.

Alternatively, a hole can be drilled at that location, or a hole could be drilled at the bottom of the finished wall. These options must be used only with the property owner's permission. After drilling a hole, wait a minute or two before inserting the collection tube in the wall to allow any dust to settle. The air pump is then turned on for one to two minutes, at a flow rate of 15 liters per minute. This rate is low to prevent sucking in debris.

The collector device can be a carpet-sampling cartridge or a spore-sampling device.

After the sampling is complete, the tube and the sampling device in front of the cassette are considered contaminated. They should be cleaned with a solution of water and alcohol, or discarded.

Viable (or Culturable) Sampling

Mold inspectors typically do not use viable sampling in their inspections.

A special air pump can be used to collect an air sample. Any mold spores in the sample can be deposited directly onto a culture plate. Under ideal conditions, molds take approximately seven days to germinate and grow mold spores. If mold is collected and cultured in a controlled laboratory environment, the species of the mold may be identified, and the number of mold colonies that develop on the plate can be counted. This identification process is referred to as viable testing. It takes longer than non-viable testing, since seven days of culturing is required. Viable testing may not identify dead mold spores or fragmented parts of hyphae, which may cause health problems or allergic symptoms. Viable testing can be expensive.

Viable or culturable sampling refers to collecting mold spores using a method that allows the spores to grow. The laboratory analyzes the samples while they are living and growing, and this allows the laboratory to accurately determine the exact type of species and genus.

Viable spore sampling is more time-consuming than a tape-lift sampling system because it depends on fungal growth.

The equipment required to capture and sustain live mold varies. A typical sampling method is to use a device that combines a sample collector, such as a cotton swab or plastic loop, with a stabilization media for transport. It captures mold spores using inertia and impacts the mold particles onto a plate coated with agar or an inert media prepared for culture at the laboratory. The mold spores grow on the plate. The sample is sent to the laboratory. The sample requires freezing or refrigeration in order to be shipped to the laboratory, and it needs to reach the laboratory within 24 hours after collection. The laboratory should be consulted about the proper collection and shipping methods prior to taking any samples.

The sample is incubated for several days to allow cell growth and replication into visible colonies. The laboratory uses a microscope to provide an accurate identification and count of the mold. The entire colony, not just the spore, is used for identification, allowing the lab to make a more precise, accurate identification of mold types and species. *Aspergillus flavus*, *Aspergillus versicolor*, *Aspergillus fumigatus*, and *Aspergillus niger* are examples of species identified using viable testing. An example of non-viable testing by the laboratory would be the determination of the *Aspergillus* mold. The viable testing will precisely identify the type and species, such as *Aspergillus flavus*. *Penicillium* and *Aspergillus* have about 150 species. *Stachybrotys* has about 15 species.

Not all of the viable fungi that collect onto an agar plate will grow during incubation. As a result, the laboratory will tend to underestimate the number of total mold spores that are present. A significant percentage of the fungi will not grow because of the growing conditions. Some molds will grow very slowly or not at all on the agar. The mold spores collected may be present, but they won't be identified or counted. As an example, *Stachybotrys* needs cellulose to grow. If a malt-extract agar

(MEA) is used for sampling, and the laboratory does not identify any *Stachybotrys* in the sample, that may mean that *Stachybotrys* is present but could not be confirmed because the MEA did not support its growth.

(If collecting a sample of suspected *Stachybotrys*, contact the laboratory to determine what type of agar to use that will support collecting viable samples for growth. The better way to identify *Stachybotrys* is to simply use a non-viable collection sample because *Stachybotrys* spores are very distinctive and can be easily identified by the laboratory under a microscope. It does not require a viable sample collection.)

It is vital to understand how a laboratory identifies and counts mold in collected samples. Identifying and counting a particular type of fungi relate to the type of viable sampling devices being used. To be accurate and efficient, choosing the appropriate type of viable sampling devices is essential in order for the laboratory to accurately identify and count the type of fungi in a sample.

Non-Viable Sampling

Mold inspectors typically use non-viable sampling in their inspections.

A non-viable sample is directly examined under a microscope. The mold spores are identified and counted. Other particulates are examined and identified based on a sample's physical features, such as fibers, skin cells, and hyphae fragments. The spores alone cannot identify some molds, such as *Aspergillus* and *Penicillium*. These are reported as a group in, for example, the *Aspergillus/Penicillium* group or the *Periconial/Myxomycetes* group.

For viable or culturable sampling, the air pump needs to be able to draw at least 28 liters per minute. A rotameter can be used to measure the air flow.

If a mold sample is collected at an on-site inspection and later observed under a microscope, then the identification process is called non-viable testing. During this type of sampling, a vacuum pulls air past a slide with a sticky surface. The slide catches dust and debris floating in the air. Swabs may be used to collect samples when there is visual evidence of mold. The species is not identified. Non-viable testing is quicker than viable testing (as short as 24 hours). Non-viable testing is less expensive. Analysis includes all mold spores and hyphae fragments. Comparison of indoor and outdoor air samples may indicate elevated levels inside the building.

Section 15: Do NOT Sample for Mold

- Do not sample for mold when a person occupying the building is under a physician's care for significant health effects attributed to mold exposure. A mold inspector should not be in conflict or dispute with a health professional by confirming or denying the absence or presence of mold, or when discussing the potential health impact from mold exposure with a client. Consultation by a health expert should be recommended.

- Do not sample for mold when there is litigation being considered or in progress in relation to mold in the building. The testimony of an expert should be recommended.

- An inspector should not sample for mold when his/her own health or safety is in danger.

- Residential home inspectors should not sample for mold in a commercial or public building.

IAQ specialists or experts in the field of commercial and public building inspections should be recommended, rather than a residential property inspector trained in performing mold inspections.

Section 16: Steps of a Mold Inspection

A General Outline for Arranging, Performing and Concluding a Mold Inspection

Before the Inspection:

1. **Scheduling an inspection** is the first step to performing a successful mold inspection. When scheduling a mold inspection with a client, be sure they completely understand what services are available and what type of inspection they are contracting for. **Setting expectations** is very important when speaking to a potential client about mold inspection services. **Provide clients with readily available information** about mold and mold inspection services, such as any documents that relate to the inspection, including the IAC2 Mold Inspection Standards of Practice, a copy of the Mold Inspection Agreement, and a sample report. Having a **company website** that includes all pertinent information, along with downloadable documents related to the inspection service, is a highly effective means of marketing and communication.

2. **Ask for** the proper spelling of the client's name, their current address, contact phone number and email address. Ask for the property address where the inspection will be performed. Set a date and time for the inspection. Request that the client attend the inspection. Get information about gaining access to the property, including the owner's name and contact information. Confirm the type of mold inspection that is being ordered by the client and the fee for the inspection.

3. **Prepare all inspection documents prior to the inspection**, including filling in the client's information on all of the documents. If the house is in the process of a real estate transaction, ask for any type of disclosure documentation provided by the owner (seller) of the property. There are several computer software companies that provide inspectors with the ability to create customized documents, templates, inspection checklists and reports. Be sure to prepare the inspection agreement and the chain-of-custody document ahead of time.

During the Inspection:

4. **Arrive at the inspection 15 minutes early**. Meet, greet, and show **proper identification** to anyone present. If the building's owner is available, **ask the following seven questions**:

    1) Are you aware of any active water penetration/intrusion at the building?

    2) Have there ever been any prior incidences of moisture or water problems in the building?

    3) Are you aware of any possible mold or mold growth in the building?

    4) Has the property ever been inspected or tested for mold or mold growth?

    5) Are any of the building's occupants presently experiencing or ever experienced their health affected by asthma, allergies or breathing problems?

    6) Are any of the building's occupants under a physician's care for significant health effects attributed to mold exposure?

    7) Is there any litigation being considered or in progress in relation to mold in the building?

5. **Explain to the client what the inspection includes**, such as what is within and beyond the scope of the mold inspection. Review the **Inspection Agreement**, allow plenty of time for the client to read and understand the agreement, have the client sign the agreement, keep the original and give them a copy.

6. **Ask the client about their concerns** with the building and the apparent condition(s) of its systems and components. Ask the client if they are aware of or suspect any conditions that have led to moisture intrusion, water damage, conditions conducive to mold growth, or the actual or apparent existence of mold growth. Develop hypotheses that can be answered by a visual examination or sampling.

7. **Perform a non-invasive examination** of the building's visible and readily accessible systems and components, in accordance with the IAC2 Mold Inspection Standards of Practice.

8. **Document your examination** using notes, sketches, checklists, digital pictures and/or computer software.

9. **Take mold samples** (air and/or surface), according to the IAC2 Mold Inspection Decision Chart and the IAC2 Mold Sampling Procedures.

10. **When you leave the building**, make sure it is in the same condition as it was when you arrived. Pick up all trash that may have come from using the mold collection devices, including wrappers, tape and latex gloves.

11. **Thank the client.** Inform them of the average turnaround time of the laboratory results, and when the inspection report will be available.

After the Inspection:

12. **Review all samples** and identification numbers. Verify possession of all samples, and make sure all samples are properly labeled and identified. Complete the chain-of-custody document for the laboratory.

13. **Send the samples to the laboratory** for analysis. Typically, this requires an overnight mailing.

14. **Retrieve** your laboratory analysis report.

15. **Prepare your inspection report** for your client. The inspection report may be generated on company letterhead, and include a description of the type of mold inspection that was performed, the scope of the mold inspection, a summary of the inspection (written in simple language that the client can understand), the actual report from the laboratory, any digital photos taken during the inspection, and instructions for obtaining additional relevant information.

16. **Deliver the report** to the client and be available for questions and further assistance.

Section 17: Interpretation of Lab Results

A laboratory report should include the laboratory's letterhead and bear the signature of a quality assurance manager of some type. A laboratory report typically consists of three parts. The first part contains the identification of the mold spores collected. Also included is a table listing spore identifications and counts.

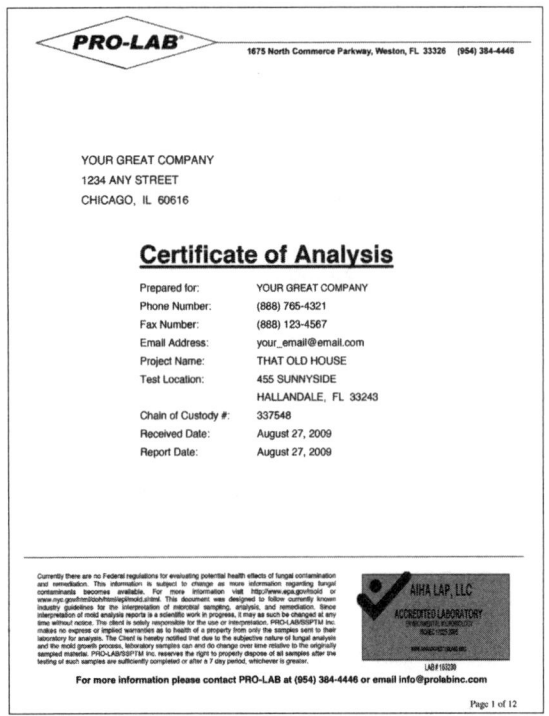

The report continues with a colored bar chart identifying spores and counts.

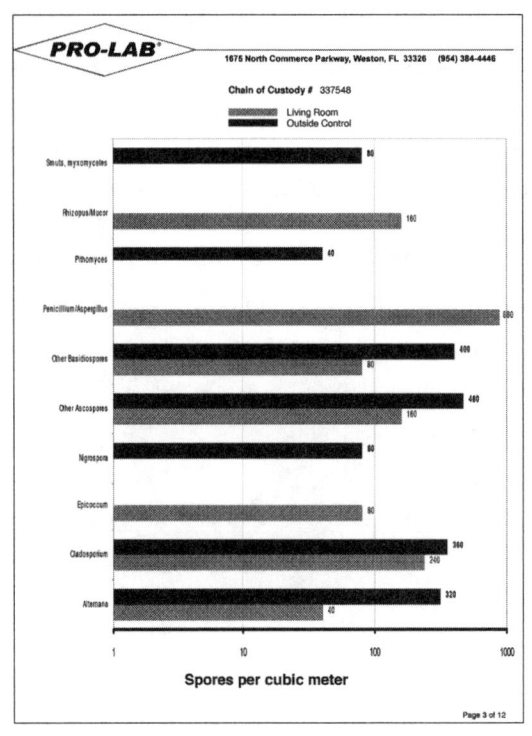

The second part of the lab's analysis contains general characteristics of mold with respect to the most common impact on human health. Many genera of molds have species with varying characteristics.

PRO-LAB® 1675 North Commerce Parkway, Weston, FL 33326 (954) 384-4446

Identification	Outdoor Habitat	Indoor Habitat	Allergic Potential	Pathogenicity	Toxins Produced	Comments
Alternaria	One of the most commonly reported airborne spores worldwide; Soil, dead or dying plants, foodstuffs, textiles	Wallboard paper backing, wood, other various cellulose-containing materials. Common in settled dust on carpets, drapes, textiles, etc.	Common allergen. Type I allergies (hay fever and asthma), Type III hypersensitivity pneumonitis. Common cause of extrinsic asthma.	Alternaria species are emerging as pathogens in immunocompromised persons.	Dextruxin B, alternariols, altenuenes, altertoxins, tenuazonic acid	Alternaria is commonly found in elevated numbers on wet-intruded building materials and in higher spore numbers in the air with respect to the outside when growth on wet building materials occurs.
Cercospora	Common everywhere, especially growing on leaves.	Not known to grow indoors.	None known.	None known.	None known.	
Chaetomium	Common everywhere growing on dung, dead leaves, wood.	Cellulose substrates, especially wallboard and wood.	Type I (hay fever and asthma) allergies.	Uncommonly seen infecting humans, but some cases have been reported mostly on immunocompromised persons.	Produces chaetoglobosins, and rarely sterigmatocystin.	
Cladosporium	The most common spore type reported in the air worldwide. Found on dead and dying plant litter, and soil.	Commonly found on wood and wallboard. Commonly grows on window sills, textiles and foods.	Type I (hay fever and asthma), Type III (hypersensitivity pneumonitis) allergies.	Human infection reported to be keratitis, and skin lesions. Other forms of infection rarely reported.	Cladosporin, emodin.	A very common and important allergen source both outdoors and indoors.
Curvularia	Commonly found everywhere on soil and plant debris.	Capable of growing on many cellulytic substrates like wallboard and wood.	Type I (hay fever and asthma) and common cause of allergenic sinusitis.	Mostly a problem in immunocompromised persons, and a common cause of sinusitis, but has been reported to cause mycetoma, onychomycosis and peritonitis.	None known.	
Epicoccum	Commonly found everywhere. Grows on plant debris, insects and soil.	Capable of growing on several different substrates, notably wallboard and paper.	Type I (hay fever and asthma) allergies.	None known.	Epicoraxine A&B, flavipin.	Very common in the summer, especially in the midwest and during harvest time.
Ganoderma	Common everywhere growing on hardwood trees.	None known.	None known.	None known.	None known.	
Memnoniella	Common everywhere in plant litter and soil.	Wet wallboard and other cellulytic substrates.	None known.	None known.	Trichothecenes, griseofulvin.	

Page 5 of 12

This report from PRO-LAB® contains comprehensive general information about indoor air-quality testing, mold testing methods, data interpretation, and symptoms of mold exposure.

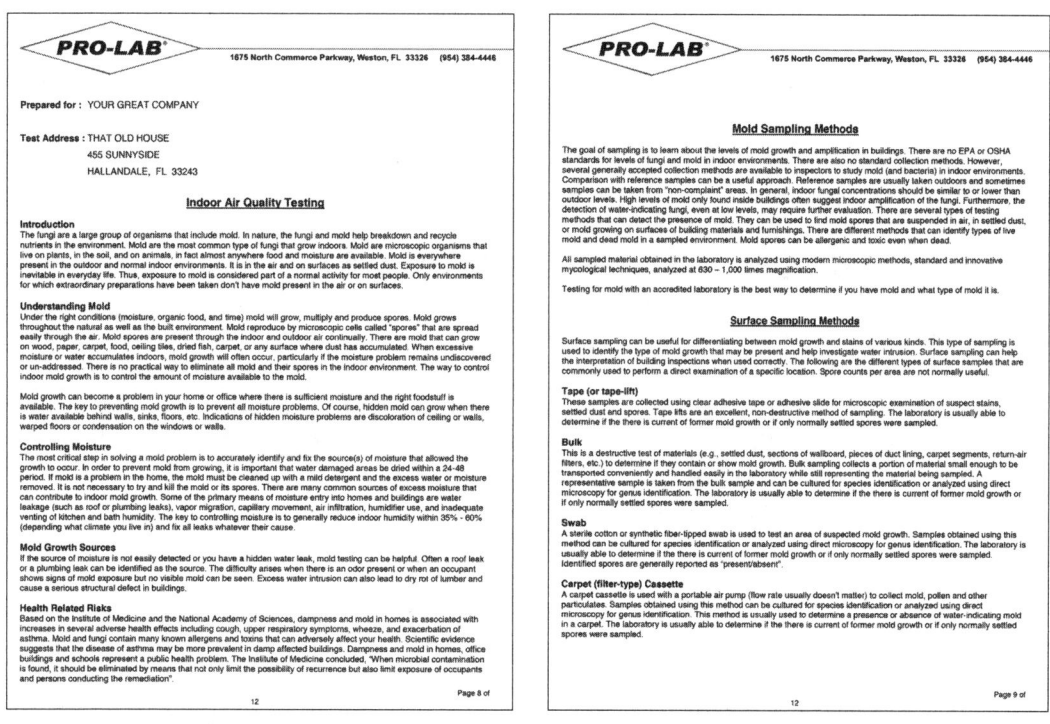

The report also includes a list of references and resources for additional information for the report's recipient.

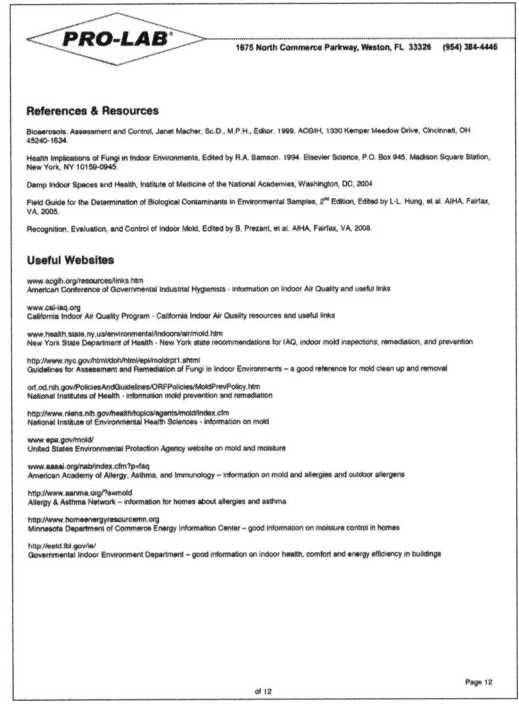
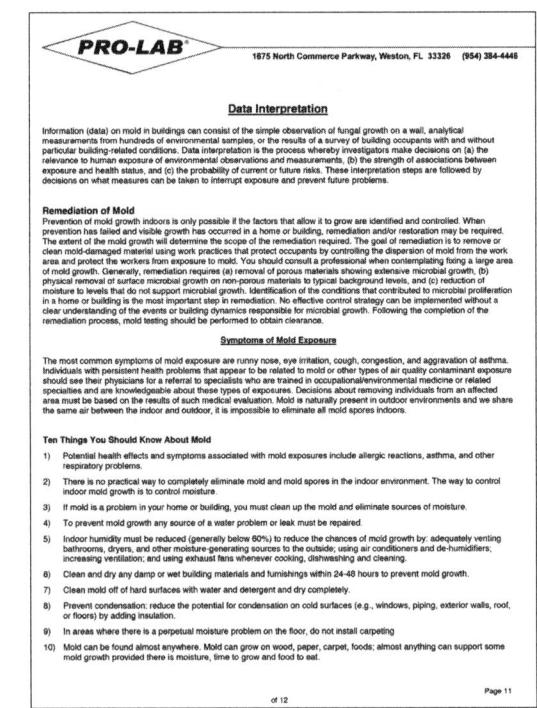

The third part of the laboratory report will include a conclusion or summary of the test's findings.

Every laboratory report should indicate whether the analysis suggests that unusual mold conditions exist or not. This determination is based upon the type of mold detected in the samples. For air-pump samples, the type of mold, as well as the indoor and outdoor counts, are considered.

Guidelines for Interpreting Laboratory Results

There have been studies of mold in homes that have provided new information about what is normal or unusual in a healthy home. Every building has mold, but deductions may be made about whether a particular building has unusual conditions or levels that may necessitate further investigation. Air samples should be evaluated by means of comparison (for example, indoors to outdoors), and by fungal type (by genera and species). In general, the levels and types of fungi found should be similar indoors as compared to the outdoor air. Differences in the levels or types of fungi found in air samples may indicate that moisture sources and the resultant fungal growth may be problematic.

Simple Confirmation

The information expected from contact surface samples is often simple confirmation that the collected material was biological in nature, or that biological growth can be ruled out.

Mold Growth Is Undesirable

Many fungi produce allergens, and some fungi produce toxins. Fungal growth in buildings is not desirable. It may cause health problems for a building's occupants. Visible, apparent mold, mold-damaged materials, and moldy odors should not be present in a healthy building. Mold growth in a building is inappropriate and should be removed. Steps should be taken to address the conditions that led to the mold growth in the first place so that it does not occur again.

Visible, apparent mold that is confirmed by a surface sampling to be actual fungal growth (mold) is evidence of indoor contamination. Air sampling may indicate indoor fungal growth that is either visible or possibly hidden. When a swab, carpet, tape, or bulk sample contains spores of any mold, then the report should indicate that unusual conditions exist.

Health Effects

It is not the mold inspector's responsibility to establish that exposure to mold spores has occurred, or that exposure is a health hazard to the client. Information on cause-and-effect relationships between biological materials and illness is not currently available.

Comparisons Should Be Similar

The kinds and concentrations of mold and mold spores in a building should be similar to those found outside. In cases when a particularly toxic mold species has been identified or is suspected, a more cautious or conservative approach to remediation is indicated.

If an air sampling shows that the types and concentrations of mold from indoor air samples are not similar to those in local outdoor air, then there is a mold problem in the building. If the indoor concentration levels exceed the outdoor levels, or when the types of mold indoors differ from those outside, then there is a mold problem in the building.

Once the mold problem is identified, and the mold remediation is completed, then the type of mold and the concentration levels of mold indoors from indoor air samples should be similar to those in the local, outdoor air.

Elevated Indoor Levels

When an air-pump sample of a building's interior contains more mold spores than an outdoor air sample, then the report should indicate that elevated conditions exist at the building, and the levels may necessitate further investigation.

Sampling Results

Hypotheses should be answered. Mold inspectors should consider the results of surface and air sampling in conjunction with the building's condition to decide if the information supports the hypotheses that have been developed, and if the information warrants a recommendation for mold remediation.

In general, immediate remediation is needed for microbial growth found on materials that are in direct contact with indoor air, or subject to disturbance that might release biological particles, as well as for materials that a building's occupants may come in contact with directly.

If sampling cannot be done properly, or if enough samples required to answer the client's concerns cannot be taken, then it is preferable not to sample at all. Inadequate sample plans may generate misleading, confusing and useless results. Samples should be analyzed according to the analytical methods recommended by the American Industrial Hygiene Association (AIHA), the American Conference of Governmental Industrial Hygienists (ACGIH), or other professional guidelines.

Keep in mind that air sampling for mold provides information only for the moment when the sampling took place. For someone without experience, sampling results will be difficult to interpret. Experience in interpreting results is essential.

Quiz on Section 17

1. T/F: There have been studies of mold in homes that have provided new information about what is normal or unusual in a healthy home.

    ☐ True
    ☐ False

2. T/F: In general, the levels and types of fungi found should be significantly different indoors as compared to outdoors.

    ☐ True
    ☐ False

3. T/F: The information expected from contact surface samples is often just simple confirmation that the collected material is biological in nature, or that biological growth can be ruled out.

    ☐ True
    ☐ False

4. T/F: Visible, apparent mold, mold-damaged materials, and moldy odors should not be present in a healthy building.

    ☐ True
    ☐ False

5. T/F: Information on cause-and-effect relationships between biological materials and illness is not currently available.

    ☐ True
    ☐ False

6. T/F: Samples should be analyzed according to the methods recommended by the American Industrial Hygiene Association (AIHA), the American Conference of Governmental Industrial Hygienists (ACGIH), or other professional guidelines.

    ☐ True
    ☐ False

7. T/F: It is the mold inspector's responsibility to establish that the client has been exposed to mold spores or that the client's exposure is a health hazard.

    ☐ True
    ☐ False

Answer Key is on page 151.

Section 18: Threshold Limit Values

Threshold Limit Values (TLV) and Guidelines

Threshold limit values (TLVs) refer to air concentrations of substances, and represent conditions under which, it is believed, people may be repeatedly exposed, day after day, without adverse health effects. But sufficient information is not currently available to formulate conclusive standards. There are no mandatory limits against which inspectors can compare measurements of air- or surface-sampling concentrations in order to correlate or connect negative health effects to mold exposure. Data on the range of inhalation exposures to mold are limited, and the methods that inspectors use to collect and analyze microbial growth (mold) vary widely.

Even if limits were set, they would be arbitrary standards because the data for any cause-and-effect relationships on which to base limits for mold exposure are few and inconsistent. The problem lies in the fact that biological exposures are often very complex mixtures of variable composition. Qualitative and quantitative information about mold (biological) exposure and any negative health effects is often imprecise because it is difficult to isolate biological materials, and the presence of materials other than those intended to be sampled could contribute to some of the health symptoms manifested by the exposed person.

Although the issue of whether exposure to indoor fungi causes adverse health effects is controversial, there is no doubt that a severely mold-contaminated building can suffer structural damage, and that a foul-smelling, fungus-filled building is aesthetically unpleasing. Controversies about health effects aside, the latter two concerns are sufficient to merit a Complete Mold Inspection and remediation when an environment is found to have fungal contamination.

People who have concerns about structural damage or the aesthetic effects of indoor fungi should seek the services of a certified mold inspector. People who have concerns about health effects of mold exposure should seek the advice of a healthcare professional.

Section 19: Mold Inspection Report

Every mold inspection report should contain information in a format that is useful to the person who needs the results. The following information should be included in a mold inspection report.

Scope of Work

The Scope of Work should list all of the hypotheses (concerns), along with a description of the sampling performed to test them. It should refer to the IAC2 Mold Inspection Standards of Practice.

Property Information

This information should include the property's address, size, age, number of occupants, and the date of the inspection. The weather conditions should be included, as well.

Visual Examination

The systems and components of the building that were inspected should be listed here. Each system and component inspected should be identified with a description. The report should include any moisture intrusion, water damage, apparent mold growth, musty odors, and conditions conducive to mold growth. A summary of the visual examination should be listed.

Sampling

The instruments and devices used in the collection of samples should be listed and described. The sampling locations identified by the areas of the building should be recorded.

Laboratory Results

A summary of the laboratory results could be written in the report. Interpretation of the results and recommendations should be confined to those that are supported directly by data obtained during the visual examination. Determination of a person's sensitivity to fungi, and the assessment of the relationship between that sensitivity and a person's symptoms, should be determined by healthcare professionals guided by the results of the mold samples taken by a mold inspector. It is not the inspector's responsibility to correlate mold in a building to the client's health.

Quiz on Section 19

1. T/F: The Scope of Work should list all of the hypotheses (concerns), along with a description of the sampling that was performed in order to test them.

    ☐ True
    ☐ False

2. T/F: The report should include the property's address, size and age of the building, the color of the entry door, number of occupants, and the date of the inspection.

    ☐ True
    ☐ False

3. T/F: The weather conditions should not be included in the report.

    ☐ True
    ☐ False

4. T/F: The sampling devices and sampling locations should be recorded in the report.

    ☐ True
    ☐ False

5. T/F: Interpretation of the results and recommendations should be confined to those that are supported directly by data obtained during the visual examination.

    ☐ True
    ☐ False

Answer Key is on page 152.

Section 20: Remediation

Mold should not be permitted to grow indoors. Problems associated with mold have been around since recorded history. As we can read in the Bible, the method in dealing with mold has changed very little for thousands of years. Solving mold problems still requires fixing the source of moisture and removing any contaminated components.

Leviticus 14:39-47: *The priest shall come again on the seventh day and shall look; and if the disease has spread in the walls of the house, he shall command that they take out the diseased stones and cast them into an unclean place outside the city. He shall cause the house to be scraped within round about and the plaster or mortar that is scraped off to be emptied out in an unclean place outside the city. And they shall put other stones in the place of those stones, and he shall plaster the house with fresh mortar. If the disease returns, breaking out in the house after he has removed the stones and has scraped and plastered the house, then the priest shall come and look, and if the disease is spreading in the house, it is a rotting or corroding leprosy in the house; it is unclean. He shall tear down the house—its stones and its timber and all the plaster or mortar of the house—and shall carry them forth out of the city to an unclean place. Moreover, he who enters the house during the whole time that it is shut up shall be unclean until the evening. And he who lies down or eats in the house shall wash his clothes.*

Leviticus 13:47-50: *The garment also that the disease of leprosy is in, whether a wool or a linen garment, whether it be in woven or knitted stuff or in the warp or woof of linen or of wool, or in a skin or anything made of skin, if the disease is greenish or reddish in the garment, or in a skin or in the warp or woof or in anything made of skin, it is the plague of leprosy; show it to the priest. The priest shall examine the diseased article and shut it up for seven days.*

Dry Quickly

Dry items before mold grows, if possible. Mold can grow instantly if there is adequate temperature, moisture and nutrients provided.

To dry carpet and backing within 48 hours, remove all water with a wet-dry vacuum, pull the carpet and pad off the floor, and dry them using a fan to blow air over them. A dehumidifier can be used to reduce the humidity in the room where the carpet and backing are drying, while fans can be used to accelerate the drying process.

Water can be removed from concrete or cinder block surfaces with a water-extraction vacuum. Dehumidifiers, fans and heaters can also be used to accelerate the drying process. Hard surface flooring (such as linoleum, vinyl and ceramic tile) should be vacuumed or damp-wiped with a mild detergent, and allowed to air-dry. They should be scrubbed clean, if necessary. If the under-flooring is wet, it should be dried using a vacuum or by exposing it to the air.

Non-porous, hard surfaces, such as plastics and metals, should be vacuumed or damp-wiped with water and a mild detergent, and then allowed to air-dry. Scrubbing may be necessary to thoroughly clean the surfaces. Water should be removed from upholstered furniture with a water-extraction vacuum. Fans, dehumidifiers and heaters may be used to accelerate the drying process. Completely drying upholstered furniture within 48 hours may be difficult, so if the piece is valuable, consider consulting a restoration or water-damage professional who specializes in furniture.

Drywall, also known as gypsum board or gypsum wallboard, may be dried in place if there is no obvious swelling and the seams are intact. Otherwise, removal is necessary. The wall cavity is the most difficult area to dry, and it should be ventilated if the drywall is left to dry in place. (Drywall is not made out of boards of wood; traditionally, drywall is made of the mineral gypsum with a layer of heavy paper on the outside and inside. Commercial gypsum boards and drywall are also available with a variety of outside layers and coatings. According to the U.S. Geological Survey, a typical new home contains more than 7 metric tons of gypsum.)

To clean water-damaged window drapes, follow the manufacturer's laundering or cleaning instructions.

To clean wooden surfaces, remove moisture immediately and use dehumidifiers, fans and gentle heat to dry them. (Be very careful when applying heat to hardwood floors.) Treated or finished wood surfaces can be cleaned with mild detergent and clean water, then allowed to air-dry. Wet paneling should be pried from the wall for drying.

Some water-damaged items, including ceiling tiles, cellulose and fiberglass insulation, drywall and gypsum board, and books and papers, may have to be discarded. If valuable or important books, documents or other items are moldy or water-damaged, consult a restoration, water-damage or remediation expert.

These guidelines are for addressing damage caused by clean water. If you know or suspect that the water is contaminated with sewage or with chemical or biological pollutants, then OSHA requires PPE and containment. An experienced professional should be consulted if the remediators do not have expertise in remediation of contaminated-water situations. Do not use fans until it is determined that the water is clean or sanitary.

Assessing a Mold Problem

Before planning a remediation effort, the size and extent of the mold problem, and any ongoing moisture problems, should be assessed. Remediation generally can be divided into small (less than 10 square feet of mold), medium (10 to 100 square feet of mold), and large jobs (more than 100 square feet of mold). A remediation manager should be selected for medium or large jobs. An experienced health and safety professional in remediation projects should be consulted, particularly on large or complex jobs.

Questions to consider before starting remediation:

- Are there existing moisture problems in the building?
- Have building materials been wet longer than 48 hours?
- Are there hidden sources of water, or is the humidity high enough to cause condensation?
- Are the building's occupants reporting musty or moldy odors?
- Are the building's occupants reporting health problems?
- Are the building's materials or furnishings visibly damaged?
- Has maintenance been delayed or has the maintenance plan been altered?
- Has the building been remodeled recently, or has its use changed?
- Are consultations with healthcare professionals indicated?

Remediation Plan

The highest priority in a remediation is to protect the health and safety of the building's occupants and the remediation workers. Remediation plans vary according to the size and complexity of the job. The plans may require updating if circumstances change or if more extensive contamination is discovered.

The remediation plan should include:

- whether containment will be required;

- what level of PPE will be used;

- how the water or moisture problem will be fixed so the mold problem does not recur; and

- how the moldy building materials will be removed to avoid spreading mold.

Mold Remediation Procedures

A variety of methods is available to remediate damage to buildings and furnishings caused by moisture-control problems and mold. The procedures selected depend on the size of the moldy area and the type of contaminated materials. Budget may also be a concern. The methods presented in this section outline one approach; some professionals may prefer to use other methods. If possible, remediation activities should be scheduled during off-hours when building occupants are less likely to be affected.

Cleanup methods may include:

Wet Vacuum

Wet vacuums ("wet-vacs") and water-extraction vacuums are designed to collect water. They can be used to remove water that has accumulated on floors, carpets and hard surfaces. Wet vacuums should be used only when materials are still wet; otherwise, they may spread mold spores. Wet vacuums alone will not dry carpets. Wet carpets must be pulled up and dried, and then reinstalled. The carpet padding must also be dried. The tanks, hoses and attachments of wet vacuums should be thoroughly cleaned and dried after use because mold and mold spores may stick to their surfaces.

Damp Wipe

Mold can generally be removed from hard surfaces by wiping or scrubbing with water and detergent. Always follow the cleaning instructions on product labels. Surfaces cleaned by damp wiping should be dried quickly and thoroughly to discourage further mold growth. Porous materials that are wet and have mold growing on them may have to be discarded. Because mold will infiltrate porous substances and grow on or fill in empty spaces and crevices, completely removing mold can be difficult, if not impossible. Mold can also cause staining and other cosmetic damage.

HEPA Vacuum

High-efficiency particulate air (HEPA) vacuums are recommended for the final cleanup of remediation areas after materials have been thoroughly dried, and contaminated materials have been removed. HEPA vacuums are also recommended for cleaning up dust that has settled outside the remediation area. When changing the vacuum filter, workers should wear PPE to prevent exposure to mold that has been captured in the vacuum. (See Section 6.) The filter and contents of the HEPA vacuum must be disposed of into well-sealed plastic bags. Care must be taken to ensure that the new filter is properly seated on the vacuum so that there are no leaks.

Throw Away Damaged Materials

Mold-contaminated building materials that cannot be salvaged should be double-bagged in 6-mil or thicker polyethylene bags. The bagged materials usually can be discarded as ordinary construction waste. Packaging mold-contaminated materials in sealed bags before removing them from the containment area is important to minimize the spread of mold spores throughout the building. Large items that have heavy mold growth should be covered with polyethylene sheeting and sealed with duct tape before being removed from the containment area.

Biocides

Biocides are substances that can destroy living organisms. The use of a biocide or a chemical that kills organisms such as mold (chlorine bleach, for example) is not recommended as a routine practice during mold cleanup. There may be instances, however, when professional judgment indicates their use (for example, when immune-compromised individuals are present). In most cases, it is not possible or desirable to sterilize an area; a background level of mold spores will remain, but these spores will not grow if the moisture problem has been resolved. If disinfectants or biocides are used, always ventilate the area and exhaust the air to the outdoors. Never mix chlorine bleach with other cleaning solutions or with detergents that contain ammonia because toxic fumes could be produced.

Note that dead mold is allergenic and may cause allergic reactions and other health effects in some individuals, so it is not enough to simply kill the mold. It must also be removed.

Floods

Buildings that have been heavily damaged by floodwaters should be assessed for structural integrity and then remediated by experienced professionals. Please note that the information covered in this manual was developed for inspecting water damage and moisture/mold conditions caused by clean water, and not flood water, sewage or other contaminated water. Visit the EPA's website at **www.epa.gov/mold/flood**, which has an EPA Fact Sheet titled "Flood Cleanup: Avoiding Indoor Air Quality Problems."

During a flood cleanup, the indoor air quality in your home or office may appear to be the least of your problems. However, failure to remove contaminated materials and reduce moisture and humidity can present serious, long-term health risks. Standing water and wet materials are a breeding ground for micro-organisms, such as viruses, bacteria and mold. They can cause disease, trigger allergic reactions, and continue to damage materials long after the flood.

Section 21: Remediation of Large Areas

For large or complex mold remediation jobs (over 100 square feet of mold growth), consider hiring professionals who have experience working on large mold remediation projects, particularly since extensive containment and PPE may be needed. Be sure to check references and ensure that the professional has experience working in mold remediation situations. Remediators should follow EPA mold remediation guidance or other governmental or professional remediation guidance. Building occupants need to be informed about what is going to happen, when it will happen, and how they may be affected.

Containment should be designed to prevent the movement of mold spores from one area of the building to another. This effort usually requires full containment using double layers of polyethylene sheeting and fans to create negative air pressure. A decontamination chamber or airlock should be used to separate the clean areas from the contaminated areas during entry into and exit from the remediation area. The entryways to the airlock from the outside, and from the airlock to the main containment area, should consist of a slit with covering flaps on the outside surface of each entry.

Full PPE may also be necessary during these operations and may consist of protective clothing and full-face or powered-air purifying respirators (PAPR) with HEPA filters. Protective clothing should include head and foot coverings with all gaps sealed with duct tape or the equivalent. Contaminated PPE, except respirators, should be removed and then sealed in bags while still inside the containment's exit chamber. Workers should wear respirators until they are in the uncontaminated area where the respirators can be safely removed. Disposable respirators can be thrown away, and re-usable respirators can be put into a bag for cleaning.

Section 22: Remediation in HVAC Equipment

Mold remediation involving a heating, ventilation and air-conditioning (HVAC) system should be performed only by professionals experienced in working with HVAC systems. Professionals may have several different methods and techniques for approaching HVAC remediation. As with the rest of a mold remediation project, professional judgment is required when working with HVAC systems, and professionals may use materials, methods and techniques not mentioned in this guide.

An HVAC system found to be contaminated with mold should be turned off and not used until the system has been remediated; using a mold-contaminated HVAC system may spread mold throughout the building and increase the exposure to the building's occupants. (There may be some exceptions or instances when all or part or the HVAC system can be run, based on professional judgment, if there is no risk of increasing occupants' or workers' exposure.) If possible, the HVAC system should be remediated during off-hours when the building is not in use.

Effective containment of the area served by the ventilation system is important to avoid the spread of mold and mold-contaminated materials. All intakes and supply vents should be sealed with plastic and tape, and negative air pressure should be maintained in work areas. (A fan can be used for this.) Contaminated, porous materials in the HVAC system should be bagged and removed. Materials that can be cleaned should be vacuumed with a HEPA vacuum or cleaned with a damp cloth and detergent solution. All items should be dried promptly.

If considering duct cleaning, first consult the EPA's guide: "Should You Have the Air Ducts in Your Home Cleaned?"

Section 23: Remediation of Confined Spaces

Confined spaces include pipe chases (areas within and under buildings where steam and utility pipes are run), and valve pits (areas below grade that contain utility shut-off valves). Working in confined areas presents numerous challenges. Movement and communication are difficult, and, if a problem arises, immediate exit from the area may be impossible.

The air in some confined spaces may be contaminated or low in oxygen, posing significant health risks for workers. Efficient rescue of an injured worker may be difficult or impossible. Poor lighting may result in increased injuries. Because exposure may be greatly magnified in a confined space, workers must use a higher level of PPE than they would when working in a more accessible area.

Worker safety must be carefully considered when deciding whether to use disinfectants or biocides because confined spaces may increase the potential for exposure. In general, work in confined spaces should be conducted only by trained professionals who have the equipment required by OSHA to deal with the inherent dangers in this type of environment.

Before remediating mold in a confined space, the area should be evaluated for atmosphere and toxic substances. If there is any chance of low oxygen, the area should be tested using the appropriate equipment. The testing equipment should be kept on site and used periodically to ensure an adequate oxygen supply.

If the area is sealed off from the rest of the building to prevent the spread of mold spores, oxygen testing should be conducted again after the area has been sealed. A frequent contaminant found in crawlspaces and pipe chases of older buildings is asbestos; chemicals such as natural gas and solvents can also be present in some of these spaces. These materials must be identified and dealt with properly to prevent exposure to workers.

Once the hazards have been identified, procedures for working in the confined space should be included in the remediation plan. Special consideration should be given to determining who will be allowed into the area, how communication will be maintained, what materials can be taken into and used in the space, and what safety equipment is necessary. Only individuals trained in the hazards associated with that space should be allowed to enter. An attendant should be posted outside of the confined space's area to summon help, if necessary. The area should be well lit so that injuries can be avoided while work is conducted efficiently.

In performing the mold remediation, every effort should be made to keep dust and mold out of the air. This can be done by using a damp cloth or pad for mold removal, and by bagging the material inside the confined space for later removal.

Mold levels are likely to be high in the confined space, so PPE should be selected accordingly. Most cases will require full PPE, including skin and eye protection, and full respiratory protection using a full-face respirator or a powered air-purifying respirator (PAPR) with a HEPA filter. The presence of asbestos may require other PPE for workers, as well as monitoring and medical evaluation.

Quiz on Section 23

1. Mold can generally be removed from hard surfaces by wiping or scrubbing with
_____.

☐ alcohol
☐ a chemical solution
☐ chlorine
☐ a biocide solution

2. Mold can grow _____ if adequate temperature, moisture and nutrients are provided.

☐ quickly
☐ gradually
☐ instantly
☐ slowly
☐ upward

3. T/F: The use of a biocide or a chemical that kills organisms such as mold (chlorine bleach, for example) is recommended as a routine practice during mold cleanup.

☐ True
☐ False

4. _____ should be designed to prevent the movement of mold spores from one area of the building to another.

☐ Decontaminant
☐ Containment
☐ Decontainment

5. Because exposures may be greatly increased in a confined space, workers must use a higher level of _____ than they would when working in a more accessible area.

☐ EPP
☐ PPE
☐ PEP
☐ OPP

Answer Key is on page 152.

Section 24: Containment

The goal of containment is to limit the spread of mold throughout the building in order to minimize the exposure of remediators and the building's occupants to mold. The larger the contaminated area, and the greater the possibility that someone will be exposed to mold, the greater the need is for containment. While the size of the contaminated area generally dictates the level of containment required, the final choice of containment level should be based on professional judgment.

Heavy mold growth in a small area, for example, could release more mold spores than lighter growth in a relatively large area. In this case, the smaller contaminated area may warrant a higher level of containment.

Two types of containment are described in the EPA's mold remediation guidance: limited and full. Limited containment is generally used for areas involving between 10 and 100 square feet of mold contamination. Full containment is used when areas larger than 100 square feet are to be remediated, or in cases where it is likely that mold could be spread throughout the building during remediation.

Maintaining the containment area under negative air pressure will keep contaminated air from flowing into adjacent, uncontaminated areas and possibly spreading mold. A fan exhausted to the outside of the building can be used to maintain negative air pressure. If containment is working, the polyethylene sheeting of the containment area should billow inward on all surfaces. If it flutters or billows outward, negative air pressure and, therefore, containment have been lost, and the problem should be found and corrected before remediation continues.

Depending on the situation, professional remediators may choose to use a variety of containment methods not described in detail here. For example, a remediator repairing a large building with extensive mold damage within the walls may choose to remove the outside layer of the wall and work inward, relying on appropriate containment to ensure that mold is not spread throughout the building.

Or, to limit the amount of mold that gets into the air, a remediator may apply sticky-backed paper or a covering to a moldy wall component before removing it.

Limited Containment

Limited containment consists of a single layer of 6-mil fire-retardant polyethylene sheeting enclosing the moldy area. Access to the contained area is through a slit-entry covered by a flap on the outside of the containment area. Limited containment is generally recommended for areas involving 10 to 100 square feet of mold contamination.

In small areas, the polyethylene sheeting can be secured to the floor and ceiling with duct tape. In larger areas, a frame of steel or wooden studs can be built to hold the polyethylene sheeting. Epoxy can also be used to fasten the sheeting to the floor and ceiling.

All supply and air vents, doors and pipe chases in the containment area must be sealed with polyethylene sheeting to minimize the spread of mold and mold spores to other areas of the building. Stairs should also be sealed if a riser is missing or open. (A pipe chase is an enclosure through which pipes are run; a riser is the upright piece of a stair step, from tread to tread.)

Heavy mold growth on ceiling tiles may affect HVAC systems if the space above the ceiling is used as a return-air plenum. In such cases, containment would be installed from floor to ceiling deck. The filters in the air-handling units serving the affected area may have to be replaced, once the remediation is complete.

Full Containment

Full containment is recommended for the cleanup of mold-contaminated surface areas of more than 100 square feet, and when intense or long-term exposures are expected. Full containment measures are also recommended if it appears that the occupant's space would be further contaminated because of the likelihood of high levels of airborne dust and/or mold spores. Full containment requires double layers of polyethylene sheeting to create a barrier between the moldy area and other parts of the building. A decontamination chamber or airlock—an area with doors between the contaminated area and the clean area—should be built for entry into and exit out of the remediation area.

The entryways from the outside into the airlock and from the airlock into the containment area should be slits covered by flaps on the outside surface. The chamber should be large enough to hold a waste container and allow a worker to put on and remove personal protective equipment (PPE). All contaminated PPE, except respirators, should be placed in a sealed bag while still inside this chamber.

Respirators should be worn until remediation workers are outside the decontamination chamber.

Section 25: Remediation Clearance Inspection

How do you know when remediation is completed?

Ultimately, it is a judgment call. People should be able to occupy or work in the building without health complaints or physical symptoms. The most important action, if mold growth is to be controlled in a building, is to eliminate the source of moisture that caused the mold problem. No matter how good the mold cleanup is, if the water problem is not solved, mold will return.

Therefore, determining whether moisture in the building is being controlled is key in assessing the effectiveness of the remediation effort. If moisture is not being controlled, even removing all of the mold growing in the building will be only a temporary solution.

A visual inspection of an area that has been remediated should show no evidence of present or past mold growth. There should be no moldy or musty odors associated with the building because these odors suggest that mold is continuing to grow.

Perform a Complete Mold Inspection for Remediation Clearance

A remediation clearance inspection is simply a Compete Mold Inspection performed in accordance with the IAC2 Mold Inspection Standards of Practice. The Null Hypothesis should be developed prior to inspecting the building where remediation was completed. The null hypothesis forces an inspector to be unbiased. The inspector starts with the opinion or perspective that there exists no mold contamination problem in the building. The inspector should not expect to discover any areas of concern: no moisture intrusion detected; no water-damaged materials present; no musty odors; no apparent, visible mold (obviously); and no conditions conducive to mold growth.

For example, if an inspection is being performed after remediation is completed, and moldy, musty odors are still present in the building, then the remediation has not been effective. The inspection report must state: "The musty, moldy odors indicate that there is an active moisture intrusion problem at the building, and there is likely mold growth at the building. We performed air sampling in the room that contained the musty, moldy odors. The results are thus.... Therefore, the remediation has not been effective. There exists a mold problem at the building. Further investigation and remediation are recommended."

Keep in mind that remodeling, cleaning and/or construction may have introduced new building materials or chemicals capable of causing upper respiratory irritation that, in some individuals, may mimic the symptoms caused by exposure to mold.

How do you know when a building is cleared for re-occupation and use?

1. The water or moisture problem is completely resolved.

2. Mold removal has been completed. Use professional judgment to determine if the cleanup is sufficient. Visible mold, mold-damaged materials, and moldy odors should not be present.

3. Based on post-remediation sampling, the types and concentrations of mold and mold spores inside the building should be similar to those found outside, once cleanup activities have been completed.

4. Upon re-visiting the site(s) shortly after remediation, it should show no signs of water damage or mold growth.

5. People should be able to occupy or re-occupy the space without health complaints or physical symptoms.

6. Again, ultimately, this is a judgment call; there is no easy way to clear a remediation project without performing a follow-up Complete Mold Inspection according to the IAC2 Mold Inspection Standards of Practice.

Bio-Aerosol Sampling

Bio-aerosol sampling (air sampling for mold or other biological contaminants) usually is not necessary to determine remediation effectiveness. In fact, bio-aerosol sampling may be less effective at determining the success of remediation than visual and sensory surveys of the area.

Although sampling may be of some help in judging remediation effectiveness, remember that a negative sampling report must not be used in place of a visual survey. Factors such as barometric pressure, indoor and outdoor temperatures, activity levels, and humidity may dramatically reduce or increase the spore levels inside a building. Air sampling for mold provides information on what was in the air only for the moment when the sampling took place. It is important, therefore, that sampling not replace visual inspection.

Communicate When You Remediate

Communicating with the building's occupants is essential for successful mold remediation. Some occupants will naturally be concerned, and their concerns may increase if they believe information is being withheld. The status of the building's investigation and remediation should be openly communicated, along with information regarding known or suspected health risks.

Small-scale remediation will not usually require a formal communication process, but do be sure to take individual concerns seriously, and consider whether formal communication is required. Managers of medium or large remediation efforts should make sure they understand and address the concerns of the building's occupants, and communicate clearly what has to be done. Depending on the situation, communication methods, strategies and issues may also be handled by others, such as building owners, school principals, and public relations specialists. Some organizations or buildings may have an established communications strategy that can be used, or they may wish to develop a comprehensive strategy.

Communication techniques may include regular memos and meetings with occupants (with time for questions and answers). The communication techniques used will depend on the scope of the remediation and the level of the occupants' concerns. Tell the occupants about the size of the remediation project, the activities planned, and the schedule. Send or post regular updates on the remediation's progress. Send or post a final memo when the project is completed, and/or hold a final meeting. Try to resolve issues and occupants' concerns as they come up. When building-wide communication is frequent and open, remediation managers can spend more time resolving the mold problem and less time responding to occupants' concerns.

Communication is especially important if occupants need to be relocated during remediation. When deciding whether to relocate occupants, consider the size of the area affected, the extent and types of health effects exhibited by the occupants, and the potential health risks associated with debris and activities during the remediation. Be sure to ask about, accommodate and plan for individuals with asthma, allergies, compromised immune systems, and other health concerns. Manage the relocation process and give occupants an opportunity to participate in resolving the problem by clearly explaining the disruption of the workplace and work schedules. Notify individuals of relocation efforts in advance, if possible.

Special communication strategies may be warranted when treating a mold problem in a school. Teachers, students and their parents, and other affected groups should be notified as soon as significant issues are identified. Consider holding a special meeting so parents can learn about the problem and ask questions of school authorities, particularly if it is necessary or advisable to vacate the school during remediation.

In some cases, particularly when large areas are contaminated with mold, or complaints run high among teachers or students, it may be a good idea to hire a remediation professional who can provide expert information to concerned parents and teachers, as well as perform the remediation work. Often, giving parents and teachers access to a professional early in the investigation and during the remediation process will reduce their concerns during the latter stages of the remediation. It is important that the best information available be provided to everyone who might be affected by the investigation and remediation.

Top Tips for Communicating with Affected Parties

- Establish that the health and safety of the building's occupants are top priorities.

- Demonstrate that the occupants' concerns are understood and taken seriously.

- Clearly present the current status of the investigation or remediation efforts.

- Identify a person whom building occupants can contact directly to discuss questions and comments about the remediation activities.

Please note: The EPA does not regulate mold or mold spores in the air. The EPA does not certify mold remediators or inspectors.

Section 26: Preventing Mold Growth

Keep the building and furnishings dry. When things get wet, dry them quickly (within 24 to 48 hours). Perform routine cleaning, maintenance and repairs. The key to mold prevention is moisture control. Water intrusion into a building or a building's crawlspaces should be controlled. If water enters a building through a leaking roof or because of a flood or accident, it should be removed immediately and the affected areas should be dried out.

Hidden Areas

Special attention should be given to areas that are hidden but which might have gotten wet. Areas behind walls and in ceilings, crawlspaces and attics are frequently overlooked and not dried out sufficiently. In general, all wet areas should be completely dried within 48 hours to prevent mold from growing.

Routine Maintenance Is Important

A number of items frequently subject to mold problems should be checked and maintained routinely. Furnace humidifiers must be cleaned regularly to prevent mold and bacterial growth. Ducts in which humidifiers are installed should also be checked to ensure that water has not leaked into the furnace or filter areas. Stand-alone humidifiers should be cleaned frequently to ensure that they are not moldy. Pay special attention to any filters in the humidifier because they can become moldy, and the humidifier can spread spores throughout the area. Carpeted areas around the humidifiers should also be monitored for wetness. Humidifiers should be set to produce less than 60% relative humidity in the building. Relative humidity greater than 60% is likely to result in condensation in the building, and that can lead to mold growth.

HVAC systems should be checked routinely because mold in a ventilation system may be spread throughout the building. Drain or condensate pans should also be checked regularly because they can become reservoirs for mold and bacteria if they are not installed and maintained properly. These pans are designed to remove water produced by cooling hot air from the ventilation system. If the pans do not drain, or are not cleaned frequently, they may allow water to enter the HVAC system and contaminate the ventilation ducts in the building. The pans themselves may grow mold and allow mold spores to be spread throughout the building. Filters for the HVAC system should be kept dry and should be changed frequently.

Toilet and bathroom areas should be carefully monitored for water and plumbing leaks. Rippling wall coverings, cracked drywall tape, peeling paint, and other signs of water damage should be investigated immediately. Such signs often indicate that water has leaked somewhere, and hidden mold growth and damage are likely. Water seepage into crawlspaces and basements should also be stopped quickly to ensure that mold will not grow. Additional measures, such as installing sump pumps and/or re-grading the area around the building, should be considered to prevent future leaks. Any areas that smell moldy or musty should be investigated to ensure that water has not entered and that mold is not growing.

Buildings should be located, built, landscaped and renovated with consideration for the climate. A building that is not suited to the climate can develop moisture problems. Buildings will get wet, both inside and out, and they must be allowed to dry or mold will grow in them. Selection and location of a building's materials and furnishings should also be made with mold prevention in mind. In areas that experience frequent moisture due to rains and/or elevated levels of humidity, more mold-resistant materials should be used; for example, some woods are more resistant to mold than particleboard or pressed board.

Mold Prevention Tips:

- Moisture control is the key.

- Keep the building clean and dry. Dry any wet or damp areas within 48 hours.

- Fix leaky plumbing and any leaks in the building's envelope as soon as possible.

- Watch for condensation and wet spots. Fix the sources of moisture problems as soon as possible.

- Prevent moisture due to condensation by increasing surface temperature or reducing the moisture level in the air (humidity). To increase surface temperature, insulate or increase air circulation. To reduce the moisture level in the air, repair leaks and increase ventilation (if outside air is cold and dry), or dehumidify (if outdoor air is warm and humid).

- Keep heating, ventilation and air conditioning (HVAC) drip pans clean, flowing properly, and unobstructed.

- Vent moisture-generating appliances, such as dryers, to the outside, where possible.

- Maintain low indoor humidity, below 60% relative humidity (RH), and, ideally, between 30% and 50%, if possible.

- Perform regular building and HVAC inspections and scheduled maintenance.

- Don't let foundations stay wet. Provide drainage, and slope the ground away from the foundation.

- If you are not experienced with home and building repairs, you may want to consult a professional when making necessary repairs, or for assistance related to mold-prevention changes to your home or building.

Note:

- For large buildings: Use the EPA's I-BEAM software to help manage indoor air quality. Routine maintenance and repairs reduce the likelihood of a mold problem developing in a building.

- For schools: Use the EPA's "IAQ (Indoor Air Quality) Tools for Schools" for guidance.

Quiz on Section 26

1. T/F: The key to mold prevention is moisture control.

　☐ True
　☐ False

2. A furnace's _____ must be cleaned regularly to prevent mold and bacterial growth.

　☐ burner chambers
　☐ dehumidifiers
　☐ thermostatic controls
　☐ humidifiers
　☐ heat exchangers
　☐ ductwork

3. T/F: To prevent mold growth, air filters of an HVAC system should be kept dry and changed frequently.

　☐ True
　☐ False

4. Vent moisture-generating appliances, such as dryers, to the _____, where possible.

　☐ chimney
　☐ basement
　☐ crawlspace
　☐ outdoors
　☐ inside
　☐ other unfinished building portions

5. T/F: To prevent mold growth, do not let foundations stay wet.

　☐ True
　☐ False

6. T/F: A remediation clearance inspection is simply a Compete Mold Inspection performed in accordance with the IAC2 Mold Inspection Standards of Practice following remediation.

　☐ True
　☐ False

Answer Key is on page 152.

Section 27: Pollen and Mold Counts

The American Academy of Allergy Asthma and Immunology (AAAAI) organized the Aeroallergen Monitoring Network, which has compiled pollen and mold counts for more than 30 years. The network was established to further the science of allergies, and to contribute to the information available to physicians for the diagnosis and treatment of allergic diseases.

The Network has reported pollen and mold spore counts to the public and the media since 1992 through the National Allergy Bureau, a service established by the AAAAI. Member stations report pollen and mold counts to the NAB, which releases reports to interested media outlets and to the public through the AAAAI's website (**www.aaaai.org/nab**). Results are reported as total counts per cubic meter for tree pollen, grass pollen, weed pollen, and mold spores, along with comments about their relative amounts. This information allows allergy sufferers and their physicians to correlate symptoms and causative agents.

Accurate forecasts of counts would allow people to adjust their activities on days with predicted high counts. Forecasting involves using counts from previous years from established testing stations and factoring those measurements in with meteorological data.

Researchers involved with the network are working on better predictive models, but they want to prove their reliability before making such predictions available to the public. Until more reliable forecasts are available, people with symptoms will have to rely on trends in recent high pollen counts to alert them to take appropriate precautions for avoiding potential allergens.

Section 28: Vital Documents

Here is a list of vital documents that every mold inspector should have for reference at every inspection:

- a work ledger;

- the IAC2 Mold Inspection Standards of Practice;

- a Mold Inspection Agreement;

- an IAC2 Mold-Sampling Decision Chart;

- "Ten Questions to Ask the Building's Owner";

- a chain-of-custody form; and

- the IAC2 Mold Sampling Procedures.

A Work Ledger

A work ledger is a small book used by an inspector during a visual examination and a sampling.

During a visual examination of a building, the inspector can write down notes in the ledger and then transfer the information to the inspection report at a later time. Answers to questions asked of occupants during the examination should be documented. Sketches of the floor plans of the building can be drawn out.

During a sampling, record the sampling locations, sampling time, and information for identifying the samples. Air-pump calibrations should be done regularly, as well as once every day that an inspection is scheduled (preferably in the morning, before any air sampling is performed). The data of the last calibration should be recorded in the ledger. Other information that should be recorded includes: type of sampling device(s) used; when the air pump was turned on and off; what the air-flow rate was at the time of the inspection; when the air pump machine was last calibrated prior to the inspection; and unique identification of the sampling(s).

Clear and complete records are necessary to compile an accurate mold inspection report. The work ledger is considered a legal document that can be of great value if there are any legal investigations about the mold inspection(s).

A list of pertinent information a mold inspector may want to record in the work ledger includes:

- the collector's name;

- date and time of the sample collection;

- address of the building;

- the people present at the time of the inspection;

- sample identification number;

- sample type (air, surface, bulk);

- sample collection site (marked on a map or sketch, or a photo of the site with the equipment in place);

- weather conditions, wind direction and general velocity;

- indoor and outdoor air temperatures, relative humidity, and moisture readings;

- temperature of the substrate;

- sample device name and/or type;

- sampling pump identification numbers;

- sampling air-flow rate, sampling start and stop times, and volume of air collected;

- sample transportation method and conditions, and sample storage conditions;

- type of analysis requested; and

- date and time samples were received at the laboratory.

IAC2 Mold Inspection Standards of Practice

In the previous section, we learned about the two types of mold inspections. A mold inspection requires the inspector to perform them according to a standard. The following are the IAC2 Mold Inspection Standards of Practice.

An updated version of the IAC2 Mold Inspection Standards of Practice is available online at **www.iac2.org/sop.php**. These standards are subject to change as more credible information about fungal contaminants becomes available. The standards may be updated at any time.

Table of Contents

28.5 IAC2 Mold Sampling Procedures

  28.5.1 General Comments

  28.5.2 Air-Flow Rate

  28.5.3 Rotameter

  28.5.4 Surface Sampling

  28.5.5 Outdoor Air Sampling

  28.5.6 Indoor Air Sampling

28.6 Limitations, Exceptions and Exclusions

28.7 Definitions

28.1 Scope

28.1.1 The purpose of this standard is to provide standardized procedures to be used for a mold inspection. There are two types of mold inspections described in the IAC2 Mold Inspection Standards of Practice:

  (1) Complete Mold Inspection (Section 28.2); and

  (2) Limited Mold Inspection (Section 28.3).

28.1.2 Unless the inspector and client agree to a limitation of the inspection, the inspection will be performed at the primary building and attached parking structure. Detached structures shall be inspected separately.

28.1.3 A mold inspection is valid for the date of the inspection and cannot predict future mold growth. Because conditions conducive to mold growth in a building can vary greatly over time, the results of a mold inspection (examination and sampling) can only be relied upon for the point in time at which the inspection was conducted.

28.1.4 A mold inspection is not a home (property) inspection.

28.1.5 A mold inspection is not a comprehensive indoor air-quality inspection.

28.1.6 A mold inspection is not intended to eliminate the uncertainty or the risk of the presence of mold, or the adverse effects mold may cause to a building or its occupants.

28.2 Complete Mold Inspection

28.2.1 The inspector shall perform:

• a non-invasive, visual examination of the readily accessible, visible, and installed systems and components of the building (listed in Section 28.4 Standards of Practice);

• moisture, temperature and humidity measurements (refer to Section 28.4.8 Moisture, Humidity and Temperature); and

• mold samples according to the IAC2 Mold Sampling Procedures (refer to Section 28.5 IAC2 Mold Sampling Procedures).

28.2.2 The inspector shall report:

• moisture intrusion;

• water damage;

• musty odors;

• apparent mold growth;

• conditions conducive to mold growth;

• results of a laboratory analysis of all mold samplings taken at the building; and

• any system or component listed in Section 28.4 Standards of Practice that were not inspected and the reason(s) they were not inspected.

28.3 Limited Mold Inspection

The Limited Mold Inspection does not include a visual examination of the entire building, but is limited to a specific area of the building identified and described by the inspector. As a result, moisture intrusion, water damage, musty odors, apparent mold growth, or conditions conducive to mold growth in other areas of the building may not be inspected.

28.3.1 The inspector shall describe:

• the room or limited area of the building where the Limited Mold Inspection is performed.

28.3.2 The inspector shall perform:

• a limited, non-invasive, visual examination of the readily accessible, visible, and installed systems and components located only in the room or limited area (as described in previous Section 28.3.1); and

• mold samples according to the IAC2 Mold Sampling Procedures (see Section 28.5 IAC2 Mold Sampling Procedures).

28.3.3 The inspector shall report:

• moisture intrusion;

• water damage;

• musty odors;

• apparent mold growth;

• conditions conducive to mold growth; and

• results of a laboratory analysis of all mold samplings taken at the building.

28.4 Standards of Practice

28.4.1 Roof

I. The inspector shall inspect from the ground level or eaves:

    A. the roof covering;

    B. the roof drainage system, including gutters and downspouts; and

    C. the vents, flashings, skylights, chimneys, and any other roof penetrations.

II. The inspector is not required to:

    A. walk on any roof surface;

    B. predict the service life expectancy; or

    C. perform a water test.

28.4.2 Exterior and Grounds

I. The inspector shall inspect from the ground level:

    A. the cladding, flashing and trim;

    B. exterior doors, windows, decks, stoops, steps, stairs, porches, railings, eaves, soffits and fascias;

    C. the exterior grading surrounding the building's perimeter; and

    D. items that penetrate the exterior siding or covering materials.

II. The inspector is not required to:

    A. inspect underground drainage systems;

    B. inspect window-well drainage; or

    C. inspect defects not related to mold growth or moisture intrusion.

28.4.3 Basement, Foundation, Crawlspace and Structure

I. The inspector shall inspect:

    A. the foundation, basement or crawlspace, including ventilation; and

    B. for moisture intrusion.

II. The inspector is not required to:

    A. operate sump pumps with inaccessible floats; or

    B. inspect for structural defects not related to mold growth or moisture intrusion.

28.4.4 Heating, Cooling and Ventilation

I. The inspector shall inspect:

    A. the air handler, circulating fan and air filter;

    B. the condensate pump;

    C. readily visible ductwork;

    D. a representative number of supply and return-air registers;

    E. the central humidifier; and

F. the central air-conditioning unit.

II. The inspector is not required to:

A. inspect the air conditioning coil, if not readily accessible;

B. inspect the condensate pan, if not readily accessible;

C. test the performance or efficiency of the HVAC system; or

D. inspect the interior of the ductwork system.

28.4.5 Plumbing

I. The inspector shall inspect:

A. the readily visible main water line;

B. the readily visible water supply lines;

C. the readily visible drain, waste and vent pipes;

D. the hot water source; and

E. fixtures such as toilets, faucets, showers and tubs.

II. The inspector is not required to:

A. test the showers or tubs by filling them with water;

B. test whirlpool tubs, saunas, steam rooms or hot tubs; or

C. inspect for plumbing defects that are not related to mold growth or moisture intrusion.

28.4.6 Attic, Ventilation and Insulation

I. The inspector shall inspect:

A. the insulation;

B. ventilation of attic spaces; and

C. framing and sheathing.

II. The inspector is not required to:

A. move, touch or disturb insulation;

B. inspect for vapor retarders; or

C. break or otherwise damage the surface finish or weather seal on or around access panels and covers.

28.4.7 Interior

I. The inspector shall inspect:

A. the walls, ceilings, floors, doors and windows;

B. the ventilation in the kitchen, bathrooms and laundry; and

    C. whole-house ventilation fans.

  II. The inspector is not required to:

    A. inspect for interior defects that are not related to mold growth or moisture intrusion.

28.4.8 Moisture, Humidity and Temperature

  I. The inspector shall measure:

    A. the moisture of any room or area of the building that has moisture intrusion, water damage, moldy odors, apparent mold growth, and/or conditions conducive to mold growth;

    B. the humidity of any room or area of the building (at the inspector's discretion); and

    C. the temperature of any room or area of the building (at the inspector's discretion).

28.5 IAC2 Mold Sampling Procedures

Table of Contents

28.5.6.3 Indoor Air

28.5.6.4 Sampling

28.5.1 General Comments

- Use the IAC2 Mold Sampling Decision Chart and the IAC2 Standards of Practice to assist in deciding when and where to take samples in a building.

- Samples of the indoor air and the outside air should be taken for comparison. There should not be any mold inside the house that is not found outside. The concentration of mold inside a home should not be higher than the concentration of mold outside.

- Keep in mind that mold spores in the air being sampled can vary greatly in relation to the life cycle of the mold, atmospheric and environmental conditions, and the amount of ventilation. There is seasonal and diurnal variability in airborne mold at an indoor residential environment.

- Air sampling may be necessary if the presence of mold is suspected (if, for example, musty odors are noted) but cannot be identified by a visual examination. The purpose of such air sampling is to determine the location and/or extent of mold contamination. All mold spores have a source, and identifying the source is the goal.

- Because the outdoor sample is the control sample and is used to compare with the indoor sample, the samples should be collected as close as possible in time and under similar conditions. Air samples should be collected at the same air-flow rate, for the same duration of time, near the same height above the floor in all rooms that are sampled indoors, and using the same type of collection device.

28.5.2 Air-Flow Rate

- There are many different types of air pumps, measurement meters and spore collectors that can be used for an air sample at a mold inspection. The air pump should be adjusted to collect air at a flow rate that is recommended by the manufacturer of the collection device. The result of an air-pump sample is recorded in spores per meter, cubed (spores/m³).

- If the air-flow rate is too fast, the spores will bounce off the collector plate or slide and will not stick. If the air-flow rate is too slow, the spores float around the collector plate or slide and will not stick.

28.5.3 Rotameter

- Rotameters are air-flow meters that provide field accuracy in an easy-to-read instrument. The principle of operation is simple: air flow passes through a vertical, tapered tube and pushes a small ball or float whose diameter is slightly less than the smaller end of the tube. As the little ball rises, the clearance between the ball and the tube wall increases. The ball becomes stationary when the diameter of the tube is large enough to allow the total air flow past the ball. The flow rate is determined by the number on the tube at the middle position of the stabilized ball.

28.5.4 Surface Sampling

- Surface sampling can provide information regarding whether the visible, apparent mold is, in fact, actual microbial growth (mold) or not, measure the relative degree of the mold contamination, and can serve to confirm that the sampled mold growth may be producing mold spores in the air.

28.5.4.1 Area of Concern: Take One Sample

- If there is an area of concern (a room or area with moisture intrusion, water damage, musty odors, apparent mold growth, and/or conditions conducive to mold growth), the inspector shall take at least one surface sample in each area of concern.

- Additional surface samples may be taken at the discretion of the inspector.

28.5.4.2 No Areas of Concern: Not Required

- If there are no areas of concern (no moisture intrusion, no water damage, no musty odors, no apparent mold growth, and no conditions conducive to mold growth), the inspector is not required to perform a surface sampling.

- Surface samples may be taken in other areas of the building at the discretion of the inspector.

28.5.4.3 Swab

- A swab comes inside a plastic tube container. The cellulose swab is moistened with a liquid preservative stored in an ampoule at one end of the tube container. Any bacteria collected with the swab are transferred via the swab into a tube. The tube is sent directly to a laboratory for analysis.

- A swab provides immediate determination of the presence of fungal spores, as well as the types of fungi present.

28.5.4.3.1 Areas of Concern

- The inspector shall take at least one swab sample when a visual examination of the building reveals moisture intrusion, water damage, apparent mold growth, musty odors, and/or conditions conducive to mold growth. Additional sampling may be performed at the discretion of the inspector.

28.5.4.3.2 Sampling

- Hold the tube container so that the ampoule with the liquid preservative is at the top. Pinch the plastic tube so the liquid will flow down onto the swab. To remove the moistened swab, pull on the cap. Rub and roll the wet swab over a 1-inch-square area of the apparent mold growth. The swab should collect visible, apparent mold. Insert the swab back into the tube. Secure the cap.

28.5.4.3.3 Each Sample

- A unique sample number should be recorded for each swab sample. Write the number on the tube itself. The chain-of-custody document should have the sample number, location, date and time of the sampling.

28.5.4.3.4 Each Room

- Take the sample in each room or area where there is visible, apparent mold.

28.5.4.3.5 Each Color

- If there is apparent mold growth of different colors in the room or area, take a sample of each different-colored mold. The different colors may indicate different mold types.

28.5.4.3.6 Each Substrate

- If mold is visible on different substrates or building materials, such as wood, drywall or wallpaper, then a sample from each different material is recommended.

28.5.4.4 Tape

- A tape system provides a quick way to sample visible mold. A tape-lift system is the most common surface-sampling technique. It can be used instead of a swab sample. Many samples can be collected in a short period of time. Samples that show hyphae fragments and reproductive structures can provide proof of mold growth.

- There are many advantages of using tape-lift systems instead of regular tape. One of the most popular tape sampling products is Bio-Tape™. The Bio-Tape™ system is easier to handle, the tapes are individually numbered, it requires less laboratory preparation time, and the slides are flexible and will not break.

- The sampling result is not quantitative. The presence of fungi can be confirmed, genera can be identified, and possibly a semi-quantitative estimation of the amount of each genus can be determined.

28.5.4.4.1 Sampling

The steps for using a tape-lift system are as follows:

- remove the slide from the mailer;

- record the sample number and all other identifying information prior to taking the sample;

- peel off the protective liner from the slide to expose the adhesive;

- place the slide with the sticky side down on the contaminated area being sampled;

- press down gently and make contact (excessive pressure is not necessary);

- lift the slide from the surface and place it back into the slide mailer. Do not replace the protective liner;

- record all information on the chain-of-custody document, including the property's address, date, time and sample number; and

- mail the sample to the laboratory.

28.5.4.4.2 PPE

- Because there is direct contact with and disturbance of the contaminated area, PPE is recommended, including gloves and a respirator rated at N-95 or higher.

28.5.4.4.3 Each Sample

- A unique sample number should be recorded for each tape sample. The chain-of-custody document should have the sample number, location, date and time of the tape sampling.

28.5.4.4.4 Each Room

- Take the tape sample in each room or area where there is visible, apparent mold.

28.5.4.4.5 Each Color

- If there is apparent mold growth of different colors in the room or area, take a tape sample of each different-colored mold. The different colors may indicate different mold types.

28.5.4.4.6 Each Substrate

- If mold is visible on different substrates or building materials, such as wood, drywall or wallpaper, then a tape sample from each different material is recommended.

28.5.4.5 Carpet

- Carpeting tends to contain the history of any mold that has been growing in the building. The carpet sampling is performed to reveal previous mold problems. A carpet sampling can also reveal undetected mold growth that may have been covered over or cleaned up. Choose an area that is not heavily walked upon—an area with little foot traffic. Do not sample under furniture.

- A household vacuum cleaner and a carpet-sampling cartridge are used to vacuum a small area of the carpet. The cartridge should be inserted as deep into the pile of the carpet as possible. If the carpet has not been cleaned thoroughly prior to a sampling, it can easily hold evidence of a mold problem in the house. Even after cleaning, there can be mold spores discovered deep in the carpet.

28.5.4.5.1 Set-Up

- Insert the nylon filter into the collector nozzle. It should snap into place. Attach the device to the vacuum hose securely. An adapter may be needed. If the attachment is loose, use duct tape to make a tight connection.

28.5.4.5.2 Sampling

- Choose a 6-foot by 3-foot sampling area in front of the sofa or large chair where occupants spend a lot of time. Vacuum this area thoroughly. Next, select a 6-foot by 3-foot area in a bedroom alongside a bed. Remove the filter. Place it into the bag that came with the unit. Mail it to the laboratory.

28.5.5 Outdoor Air Sampling

28.5.5.1 Two Outdoor Samples

- The inspector shall perform two outdoor samples of the highest-quality general air to be used as control samples (or background samples). These samples are to be used for comparison with the indoor sample(s).

28.5.5.2 Upon Arrival

- The outdoor sampling should begin soon after arriving at the property, assuming that the weather is clear and calm. It is better to perform the outdoor sampling while the weather is favorable than to wait. The outdoor conditions may change drastically during the examination and sampling of the building's interior.

28.5.5.3 Weather

- Air sampling should not be conducted during unusually severe storms or periods of unusually high winds. Severe weather will affect the sampling and analysis results in several ways.

- First, a high wind will increase the variability of airborne mold-spore concentration because of wind-induced differences in air pressure between the building's interior and exterior. Second, rapid changes in barometric pressure increase the chance of a large difference in the interior and exterior air pressures, consequently changing the rate of airborne mold spores being sucked into the building. Weather predictions available on local news stations can provide sufficient information to determine if these conditions are likely.

28.5.5.3.1 Clear and Calm

- On a chain-of-custody form, the weather conditions shall be recorded. The weather conditions should be clear and calm. High winds may affect the quality of the sampling, including the comparison between indoor and outdoor sampling.

28.5.5.3.2 No Rain

- Air pump sampling should not take place outdoors if it is raining. If possible, wait for at least two hours after the rain has stopped before taking an air-pump sample. Alterations or adjustments to the normal procedure or locations of taking air-pump samples, particularly for the control sample, must be recorded on a chain-of-custody form.

28.5.5.3.3 Above Freezing

- Air-pump sampling should not take place when the outdoor air temperature is below 32° F. All air sampling should take place when the air temperature is above freezing.

28.5.5.3.4 No Snow Covering

- If the ground is completely covered with snow, outdoor air-pump sampling should not be performed. A partial covering or a light dusting of snow is acceptable.

28.5.5.3.5 Ten Minutes

- On a clear, windless day, air-pump sampling should run for 10 minutes. (Be sure to refer to the manufacturer's recommendation.) When the outdoor air is something other than clear and windless, then the time of the sampling should be reduced to five minutes or less. A breeze, the mowing of grass, nearby construction, and dusty air can all affect the sampling conditions.

28.5.5.4 Location

- If possible, one outdoor sample should be located on the windward-side of the building (the side facing the point from which the wind blows), and the other should be located on the leeward-side of the building (the side sheltered from the wind).

- The sampling device located on the windward-side of the building should be positioned so as to face the wind directly. The sampling device should point toward the wind, in the direction of the point from which the wind is blowing. The sampling device should be 3 to 6 feet from the ground's surface (the breathable space).

- Typically, the device should be located about 10 feet away from the front entry door. The idea is to have both outdoor samples located in areas where the devices will collect a representative sampling of the air that may enter the building through the entry door or nearby open windows (the openings on the sides of the building).

28.5.5.4.1 Ten Feet

- If there is a main ventilation component of the building that draws fresh air into the building from outside, sampling should be performed 10 feet from that intake.

- The sampling should be performed at least 10 feet from the most frequently used entrance to the home.

- The air sampling devices should be kept at least 10 feet away from all openings, air intakes, registers, exhaust vents, vent pipes, ventilation fans, etc.

28.5.5.4.2 Nothing Overhead

- Sampling should not be performed under an overhang, soffit or eave, carport, porch roof, or any other roof or overhead structure.

28.5.6 Indoor Air Sampling

28.5.6.1 Closed-Building Conditions

- Indoor air sampling should be made under closed-building conditions. Closed-building conditions are necessary in order to stabilize the air that may contain mold spores or mVOCs, and to increase the reproducibility of the air sampling and measurement.

- Windows on all levels and external doors should be kept closed (except during normal entry and exit) during the sampling period. Normal entry and exit include a brief opening and closing of a door, but—to the extent possible—external doors should not be left open for more than a few minutes.

- In addition, external-internal air-exchange systems (other than a furnace), such as high-volume, whole-house and window fans, should not be operating. However, attic fans intended to control attic (and not whole-building) temperature or humidity should continue to operate. Combustion or make-up air supplies must not be closed.

- Normal operation of permanently installed energy-recovery ventilators (also known as heat-recovery ventilators or air-to-air heat exchangers) may also continue during closed-building conditions. In houses where permanent radon mitigation systems have been installed, these systems should be functioning during the air-sampling period.

- Closed-building conditions will generally exist as normal living conditions in northern areas of the country when the average daily temperature is low enough so that windows are kept closed. Depending on the geographical area, this can be the period from late fall to early spring.

28.5.6.2 HVAC

28.5.6.2.1 Take One Air Sample

- At least one air sample shall be taken at an air supply register of the HVAC system. It is preferred to sample prior and during the operation of the HVAC system. If only one sampling can be performed, then the sample should be taken 15 minutes after the HVAC system is turned on.

- Ideally, there would be at least three sampling devices similarly situated throughout the building, but financial or time constraints may limit the number of samples that can be taken.

28.5.6.2.3 Location

- The air sample should be taken 3 to 5 feet from an air supply register, with the sampling device oriented so that air from the supply register directly enters the sampling device.

28.5.6.2.4 Agitation

- A gentle or vigorous mechanical agitation of the ductwork (a bump or shake) is appropriate.

28.5.6.3 Indoor Air

28.5.6.3.1 Take One Air Sample

- The inspector shall perform at least one indoor sampling. Additional samples may be taken at the discretion of the inspector.

28.5.6.3.2 Areas of Concern

- At least one air sample shall be taken near the center of each room or area of the building where there are areas of concern (moisture intrusion, water damage, musty odors, visible, apparent mold growth, and/or conditions conducive to mold growth).

28.5.6.3.3 No Areas of Concern

- At least one indoor air sample shall be taken in the most lived-in common room, such as the family room or living room. (The location shall be determined at the discretion of the inspector.)

28.5.6.3.4 Location

- An indoor air sampling should take place only in a livable space in the building. Sampling in areas such as closets, under-floor crawlspaces, unfinished attics, storage or utility rooms, or inside the HVAC system is prohibited.

- The indoor air sample should be taken in the middle or center of the area or room.

- The air collection device should be about 3 to 6 feet above the floor surface.

28.5.6.3.5 Ten Minutes

- Inside the building, the air-pump sampling should run for 10 minutes. If there is a lot of indoor activity, then the air-pump sampling should be reduced to five minutes. If there is an active source of dust, such as construction or cleaning, then the air-sampling time should be reduced to one minute. Be sure to follow the recommendations of the manufacturer of the sampling device or collector.

28.5.6.4 Sampling

- The sampling equipment must be protected, clean, and properly maintained at all times. The sampling device shall be clean and free from dirt and debris prior to starting a sample. If re-usable collection devices are used, then they shall be handled and cleaned prior to use, in accordance with the manufacturer's recommendation. The collector may be re-usable and have sticky sides already prepared, or the collector may be a one-time-use, self-contained device.

- Slides, cassettes, and one-time-use devices should be stored in cool, dry environments. The slides must be protected from direct sunlight. Sampling devices (slides, swabs, cassettes, tapes) older than one year should not be used.

- Set the air collector at a normal breathing height, which is about 3 to 6 feet above the ground level or floor's surface. A tripod is typically used to set the collector's height.

- Calibrate the flow of the pump. Do not attach the sampling device, cassette or collector on the tubing yet. Measure the flow rate of the pump with a rotameter that has been calibrated to a standard. Make sure that the flow rate is set to the manufacturer's recommendation. For example, an Air-O-Cell® cassette flow rate is 15 liters of air per minute. The pump should be calibrated regularly (once a day). A record of calibrations should be kept in a work ledger or log book.

- After calibration, securely attach the tubing of the pump to the sampling device or collector. Turn on the pump. Start sampling. Record start time.

- After turning on the air pump, check the air-flow rate. The flow rate should not vary. A flow change greater than 5% requires a new air sample to be taken. All air samples must have the same volume. A digital time controller on the equipment is highly recommended.

- Examine the collector. There should not be an overload on the slide. There should be a fine trace, hardly visible to the human eye, of dust and spores on the slide. A slide that has an obvious visible trace on it may be unreadable. If that is the case, the environmental conditions may need improvement, or a new sampling location may be needed. If a slide is heavy, a new sample should be taken.

- Remember, all air samples must have the same volume. Refer to the manufacturer's recommendations about sampling time and volume for each type of sampling device.

- Record the time that the pump stopped. Mark the sampling device with a unique sampling number. Record that information on the chain-of-custody form.

- Place slides in a protective carrying case, or close the collector, if a cassette is used. A new sample must be taken if a slide is accidentally touched, smeared, or contaminated because it will be unreadable.

- Calculate the volume by multiplying the liters of air pumped by the number of minutes. An example of the calculation is 20 liters of air pumped multiplied by 10 minutes equals 20 liters per minute or 200 liters (20L x 10 minutes = 200 L).

28.6 Limitations and Exclusions

28.6.1 Limitations

I. These Standards of Practice apply only to residential buildings with four or fewer dwelling units.

II. The mold inspection is not a warranty, guarantee or insurance policy.

III. The mold inspection is not technically exhaustive.

IV. The mold inspection will not identify concealed or latent conditions or defects.

V. The mold inspection will not identify mold growth not readily visible at the time of the inspection.

VI. The scope of a mold inspection does not include future conditions or events.

VII. The scope of a mold inspection does not include hidden mold growth, or future mold growth.

28.6.2 Exclusions

I. The inspector is not required to report:

    A. the condition of any system or component that is not readily accessible;

    B. the condition of any system or component that is not in the IAC2 Standards of Practice;

    C. the service life expectancy of any system or component;

    D. the size, capacity, BTU, performance or efficiency of any component or system;

    E. compliance with codes, regulations or installation guidelines; or

    F. the presence of evidence of rodents, animals, insects, wood-destroying insects or pests.

II. The inspector is not required to:

    A. determine the presence of hidden mold by physical examination or sampling;

    B. report replacement or repair cost estimates;

    C. lift carpeting or padding;

    D. inspect any other environmental issue;

    E. determine the cause or reason of any condition;

    F. perform a geotechnical, structural or geological evaluation;

    G. move any personal items or other obstructions to the inspection, such as, but not limited to: insulation, throw rugs, furniture, floor or wall coverings, ceiling tiles, window coverings, equipment, plants, ice, debris, snow, water, dirt, foliage or appliances;

    H. dismantle, open or uncover any system or component;

    I. enter or access any area, crawlspace or attic space, which, in the opinion of the inspector, may be unsafe or may risk personal safety;

    J. do anything that may be unsafe or dangerous to the inspector or others, or which may damage property, in the inspector's opinion; or

    K. determine the insurability of a property.

III. The inspector is not required to operate:

    A. any system that is shut down;

    B. any system that does not function properly;

    C. any system that does not turn on with the use of normal operating controls;

    D. any water shut-off or fuel valves, or manual stop-valves;

    E. any electrical disconnect or over-current protection devices; or

    F. any irrigation or sprinkler systems.

28.7 Definitions

- **accessible:** can be approached or entered by the inspector safely, without difficulty, fear or danger.

- **apparent mold:** visible growth with characteristics of mold, which cannot be confirmed by the inspector without the benefit of sampling. The term "mold growth" is interchangeable in this guide with "fungal growth" and "microbial growth."

- **area of concern:** a room or area with moisture intrusion, water damage, musty odors, visible, apparent mold growth, and/or conditions conducive to mold growth.

- **complete:** comprehensive in scope or purpose.

- **component:** a permanently installed or attached fixture, element or part of a system.

- **condition:** the visible and conspicuous state of being of an object.

- **dismantle:** to open, take apart or remove any component, device or piece that would not typically be opened, taken apart or removed by an ordinary occupant.

- **due diligence:** the degree of care and caution required by a person for the circumstances.

- **dwelling unit:** a complete place to live, including a kitchen and bathroom.

- **household appliances:** kitchen and laundry appliances, room air conditioners, and similar appliances.

- **inspect:** to visually look at readily accessible systems and components safely, using normal operating controls, and accessing readily accessible panels and areas, in accordance with these Standards of Practice.

- **inspector:** one who performs an inspection.

- **invasive:** to probe, dismantle or take apart a system or component.

- **interior:** the area(s) of a building where people have access and which are included in the living space of the building.

- **limited:** not comprehensive in scope or purpose.

- **microbial:** microscopic organism, such as mold.

- **normal operating controls:** devices such as thermostats that would be operated by ordinary occupants, and which require no specialized skill or knowledge.

- **occupants:** tenants, persons or entities, each of which uses a portion of the building.

- **readily accessible:** an item or component is readily accessible if, in the judgment of the inspector, it is capable of being safely observed without movement of obstacles, detachment or disengagement of connecting or securing devices, or other unsafe or difficult procedures to gain access.

- **report:** a written communication (possibly including digital images) of conditions observed during the inspection.

- **representative number:** at least one in a particular room or area.

- **sampling:** the collection of air, surface or carpet samples for analysis.

- **shut down:** turned off, unplugged, inactive, not in service, not operational, etc.

- **system:** an assembly of various components which function as a whole.

- **technically exhaustive:** a comprehensive and detailed examination beyond the scope of a mold inspection, which would involve or include, but would not be limited to: dismantling, specialized knowledge or training, special equipment, measurements, calculations, testing, research, analysis, or other means.

- **unsafe:** a condition in a readily accessible, installed system or component, which is judged to be a significant risk of personal injury during normal, day-to-day use. The risk may be due to damage, deterioration, improper installation, or a change in accepted residential construction standards.

Mold Inspection Agreement

InterNACHI's Mold Inspection Agreement (below) is available online at **www.nachi.org/moldagreement**

Mold Inspection Agreement

This is an Agreement ("Agreement") between _____ ("INSPECTION COMPANY") and the undersigned client ("CLIENT"), collectively referred to herein as the "PARTIES." CLIENT agrees to employ the INSPECTION COMPANY to perform a mold inspection as set forth herein.

1. Address: The address of the property to be inspected: _____ _____

2. Fee: The fee for the inspection service is $ _____ and is based on a single visit to the property. The inspection is not technically exhaustive.

3. Purpose: The purpose of the inspection is to attempt to detect the presence of mold by performing a visual inspection of the property and collecting samples to be analyzed by a laboratory.

4. Scope: The scope of the inspection is limited to the readily accessible areas of the property, and is based on the condition of the property at the precise time and date of the inspection, and on the laboratory analysis of the samples collected. Mold can exist in inaccessible areas, such as behind walls and under carpeting. Furthermore, mold grows. As such, the report is not a guarantee that mold does or does not exist. The report is only indicative of the presence or absence of mold. As a courtesy, the INSPECTION COMPANY may point out conditions that contribute to mold growth, but such comments are not part of the bargained-for report.

5. Report: The CLIENT will be provided with a written report of the INSPECTION COMPANY's visual observations, and copies of the results of the laboratory analysis of the samples collected. The INSPECTION COMPANY is not able to determine the extent or type of microbial contamination from visual observations alone. The report will be issued only after the laboratory analysis is completed. The report is not intended to comply with any legal obligations of disclosure.

6. Exclusivity: The report is intended for the sole, confidential and exclusive use and benefit of the CLIENT, and the INSPECTION COMPANY has no obligation or duty to any other party. INSPECTION COMPANY accepts no responsibility for use by third parties. There are no third-party beneficiaries to this agreement. This Agreement is not transferable or assignable. Notwithstanding the foregoing, the CLIENT understands that the INSPECTION COMPANY may

notify the homeowner, occupant or appropriate public agency of any condition(s) discovered that may pose a safety or health concern.

7. Limitation of Liability: It is understood the INSPECTION COMPANY and the laboratory are not insurers, and that the inspection, laboratory analysis and report shall not be construed as a guarantee or warranty of any kind. The CLIENT agrees to hold the INSPECTION COMPANY and their respective officers, agents and employees harmless from and against any and all liabilities, demands, claims, and expenses incident thereto for injuries to persons, and for loss of, damage to, or destruction of property, cost of repairing or replacing, or consequential damage arising out of or in connection with this inspection.

8. Limitations Period: Any legal action arising out of this Agreement or its subject matter must be commenced within one year from the date of the Inspection or it shall be forever barred. The CLIENT understands that this limitation period may be shorter than the statute of limitations that would otherwise apply.

9. Litigation: The parties agree that any litigation arising out of this Agreement shall be filed only in the Court having jurisdiction in the County where the INSPECTION COMPANY has its principal place of business. If INSPECTION COMPANY is the substantially prevailing party in any such litigation, the CLIENT shall pay all legal costs, expenses and attorney's fees of the INSPECTION COMPANY in defending said claims. The CLIENT further agrees that the International Association of Certified Home Inspectors, Inc. ("Association") is not a party to this Agreement, and any action against it or its officers, agents or employees allegedly arising out of this Agreement or INSPECTION COMPANY's relationship with the Association must be brought only in the District Court of Boulder County, Colorado. If the Association substantially prevails in any such action, the CLIENT shall pay all legal costs, expenses and attorney's fees of the Association in defending said claims.

10. Severability: If any court having jurisdiction declares any provision of this Agreement to be invalid or unenforceable, the remaining provisions will remain in effect.

11. Entire Agreement: This Agreement represents the entire agreement between the PARTIES. No statement or promise made by the INSPECTION COMPANY or its respective officers, agents or employees shall be binding.

CLIENT has carefully read the foregoing, understands it, and voluntarily agrees to it.

_____

CLIENT   (Date)

IAC2 Mold Sampling Decision Chart

Condition	Perform Swab Sampling?	Perform Tape Sampling?	Perform Indoor Air Sampling?	Perform Outdoor Air Sampling?	Perform Carpet Sampling?	Perform Wall Sampling?
visible, apparent mold	YES (or a tape sampling)	YES (or a swab sampling)	YES, in the area(s) of the building with visible, apparent mold growth	YES: two outdoor samples (one windward; one leeward)	POSSIBLY, at the discretion of the inspector	NO
no visible apparent mold, but there are condition(s) conducive to mold growth	YES (or a tape sampling) at water stains, water damage, areas of moisture, or other areas at the discretion of the inspector	YES (or a swab sampling) at water stains, water damage, areas of moisture, or other areas at the discretion of the inspector	YES, in the area(s) of the building with condition(s) conducive to mold growth	YES: two outdoor samples (one windward; one leeward)	YES, in the area(s) of the building with condition(s) conducive to mold growth	YES, at the wall with condition(s) conducive to mold growth
no visible apparent mold, and no visible conducive conditions	NO	NO	YES, near HVAC return duct (if available); otherwise, at least one sampling in the most lived-in common room (such as the family room or living room)	YES		

Ten Questions to Ask the Building's Owner

If an occupant or the owner of the building is available, ask the following 10 questions:

1) Are you aware of any active water penetration/intrusion in the building?

2) Have there ever been any prior experiences with moisture or water problems in the building?

3) Are there any active plumbing leaks?

4) Have there been any plumbing leaks that have been repaired?

5) Are there any areas of the building that have a musty odor?

6) Are you aware of any apparent mold growth (or mold) in the building?

7) Has the property ever been inspected or tested for mold growth (or mold)?

8) Are any of the building's occupants currently experiencing or ever experienced their health affected by asthma, allergies, breathing problems, or mold growth (or mold exposure)?

9) Are any of the building's occupants under a physician's care for significant health effects attributed to mold exposure?

10) Is there any litigation in progress or being considered in relation to mold in the building?

Chain-of-Custody Form

It is essential that work is documented while performing an environmental inspection and sampling. A mold inspection is meaningless if the work cannot be traced through a chain-of-custody document that identifies the date, address, sampling method and sampling location. The chain-of-custody form is considered a legal document. It must be properly and accurately completed. It must be filled out legibly; an unreadable or incomplete document can be a legal liability.

The purposes of a chain-of-custody document for samples are:

1) to ensure that field and laboratory personnel do not lose track of or exchange samples;

2) to prevent tampering with samples;

3) to track any accidental mishandling that might compromise a sample's integrity; and

4) to qualify laboratory results as evidence in legal cases.

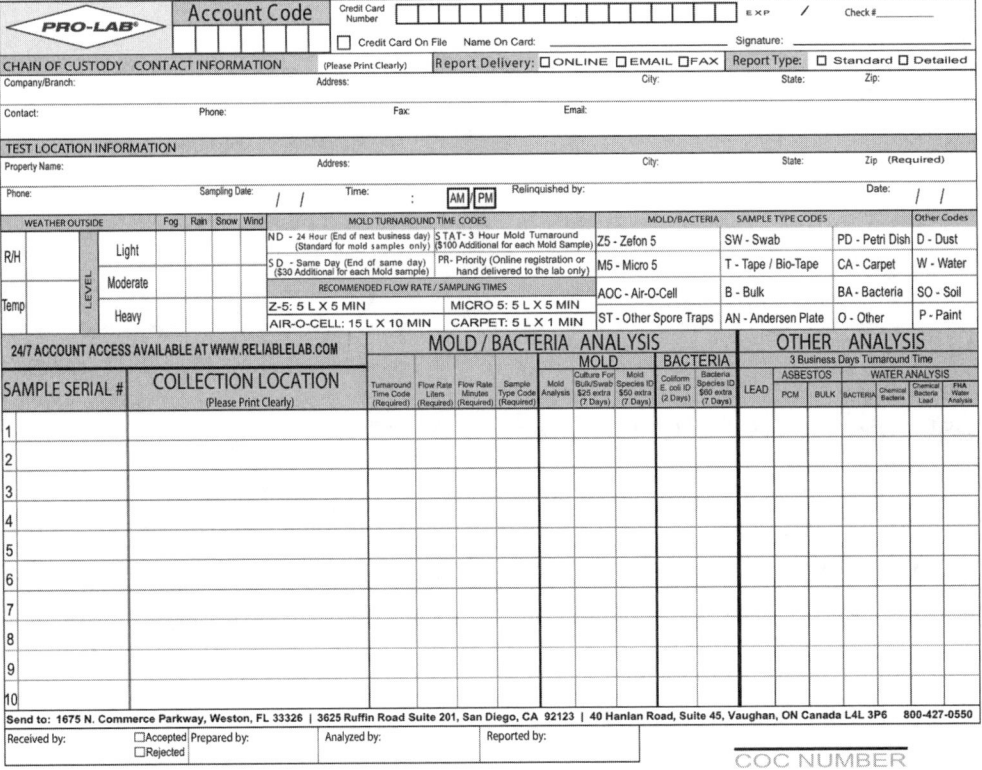

Pictured on the previous page is the chain-of-custody form from PRO-LAB®. Note the following:

A. Each sample must be marked with a unique identification number that matches the one recorded in the chain-of-custody form.

B. Air-sample volumes must be calculated and recorded. The laboratory requires this information in order to calculate spores per cubic meter.

C. Shipping samples to the laboratory via overnight delivery is typically preferred. The laboratory should be consulted about the proper collection and shipping methods prior to taking any samples.

Section 29: Glossary of Terms

- **air-handling unit (AHU):** equipment that includes a blower or fan, heating and/or cooling coils, and related equipment, such as controls, condensate drain pans, and air filters; does not include ductwork, registers or grilles, or boilers or chillers.

- **allergen:** a substance (such as mold) that can cause an allergic reaction.

- **anti-microbial:** a chemical or other agent that kills microbial growth (mold or other organisms). See also "Biocide" and "Fungicide."

- **biological contaminants:** 1) living organisms, such as viruses, bacteria, or mold (fungi); 2) the remains of living organisms; or 3) debris from or pieces of dead organisms. Biological contaminants can be small enough to be inhaled, and may cause many types of negative health effects, including allergic reactions and respiratory disorders.

- **biocide:** a substance or chemical that kills organisms, such as mold.

- **borescope:** an optical probe inserted through a small hole drilled into a wall that lets an investigator inspect a small portion of the wall's cavity without causing extensive damage.

- **building envelope:** elements of the building, including all external building materials, windows and walls, that enclose the internal space.

- **ceiling plenum:** the space between a suspended ceiling and the floor above that may have mechanical and electrical equipment in it, and that is used as part of the air-distribution system. The space is usually designed to be under negative air pressure.

- **fungi:** a separate kingdom comprising living things that are neither animal nor plant. The kingdom Fungi includes molds, yeasts, mushrooms and puffballs. In this guide, the terms "fungi" and "mold" are used interchangeably.

- **fungicide:** a substance or chemical that kills fungi.

- **HEPA filter:** high-efficiency particulate air filter.

- **HVAC:** heating, ventilation and air-conditioning.

- **hypersensitivity:** great or excessive sensitivity.

- **hypersensitivity pneumonitis:** a group of respiratory diseases that causes inflammation of the lungs (specifically, the granulomatous cells). Most forms of hypersensitivity pneumonitis are caused by the inhalation of organic dusts, including molds.

- **mold:** a group of organisms that belong to the kingdom Fungi. In this guide, the terms "fungi" and "mold" are used interchangeably.

- **mVOC (microbial volatile organic compound):** a chemical produced by mold that, at room temperature, takes the form of a gas, and may have a moldy or musty odor.

- **mycotoxin:** a toxin produced by a mold.

- **negative (air) pressure:** a condition that exists when less air is supplied to a space than is exhausted from the space, so the air pressure within that space is less than that in surrounding areas. Under this condition, if an opening exists, air will flow from surrounding areas into the negatively pressurized space.

- **plenum:** an air compartment connected to a duct or ducts.

• **pressed-wood products:** a group of materials used in building and furniture construction made from wood veneers, particles or fibers bonded together with an adhesive using heat and pressure.

• **remediate:** fix.

• **spore:** the means by which molds reproduce. Spores are microscopic. They vary in shape and range from 2 to 100 microns in size. Spores travel in several ways: passively, moved by a breeze or water drop; mechanically disturbed (by a person or animal passing by); or actively discharged by the mold (usually under moist conditions or high humidity).

• **toxigenic:** producing toxic substances.

See also: Indoor Air Quality Glossary of Terms at: **www.epa.gov/iaq/glossary.html**

Section 30: Sources and Resources

Sources Consulted:

1. Ace Laboratories, Inc., Thousand Oaks, Calif. and Entech Instruments, Inc., Simi Valley, Calif.: "Canister Sampling of mVOCs for Rapid Mold Screening" by Thomas Robinson, Daniel Cardin and Christopher Casteel (2005)

2. American Conference of Governmental Industrial Hygienists (ACGIH.org): "Bio-Aerosols: Assessment and Control" (1999)

3. American Society for Microbiology: Applied and Environmental Microbiology, American Society for Microbiology "Profiles of Airborne Fungi in Buildings and Outdoor Environments in the United States" by Brian Shelton, Kimberly Kirkland, W. Dana Flanders and George Morris. (April 2002)

4. ASTM International: "Standard Guide for Readily Observable Mold and Conditions Conducive to Mold in Commercial Buildings: Baseline Survey Process" (March 2006)

5. "The Fungi: How They Grow and Their Effects on Human Health" by Harriet A. Burge, Ph.D.

6. California Department of Health Services: Indoor Air Quality Info Sheet, "Mold in My Home: What Do I Do?" (June 2006)

7. Consumer Product Safety Commission: "Biological Pollutants in Your Home" (Publication #425);

8. "Evaluation of Fungal Growth on Fiberglass Duct Materials for Various Moisture, Soil, Use and Temperature Conditions" by Foarde, VanOsdell and Chang (November 1995)

9. Institute of Medicine: "Damp Indoor Spaces and Health" (2004)

10. The Journal of Allergy and Clinical Immunology. Volume 113, Issue 2 (February 2004)

11. Minnesota Department of Health, Environmental Health Division, Indoor Air Unit: "Recommended Best Practices for Mold Investigations in Minnesota Schools" (November 2001)

12. Mold Inspection Training Online Video Course by NACHI.TV, with comments by Dr. John Shane, PRO-LAB®'s vice president of Laboratory Services and head of PRO-LAB®'s Scientific Advisory Board (August 2008)

13. New York City Department of Health's "Guidelines on Assessment and Remediation of Fungi in Indoor Environments" (2000)

14. U.S. Environmental Protection Agency:

    • "A Brief Guide to Mold, Moisture, and Your Home";

    • "Introduction to Mold and Mold Remediation for Environmental and Public Health Professionals" (July 2008);

    • "Mold Remediation in Schools and Commercial Buildings" (March 2001);

    • "The Online Mold Course" (**www.epa.gov/mold/moldcourse**)

15. U.S. Department of Health and Human Services and the Centers for Disease Control: "Molds in the Environment" (March 2005)

Additional Resources:

- International Association of Certified Home Inspectors, Inc. (InterNACHI): **www.nachi.org**

- International Association of Certified Indoor Air Consultants, Inc. (IAC2): **www.IAC2.org**

- Moisture Meters and Infrared Cameras: **www.InspectorOutlet.com**

- Move-In Certified's free, online Green Questionnaire: **www.moveincertified.com/gogreen**

- PRO-LAB®: **www.ReliableLab.com**

- InterNACHI's free, online Mold Inspection Course: **www.nachi.org/moldcourse.htm**

- InterNACHI's online comprehensive Mold Inspection Video Course: **www.nachi.org/videomoldcourse.htm**

- InterNACHI's free, online Building Science and Thermal Imaging Course: **www.nachi.org/advancedcourses.htm**

- InterNACHI's online Building Science and Thermography Video Course: **www.nachi.org/buildingsciencethermal.htm**

- InterNACHI's free, online Moisture Intrusion Inspection Course: **www.nachi.org/moisturecourse.htm**

- InterNACHI's online HVAC Training Course: **www.nachi.org/hvacclass2008.htm**

- InterNACHI's free, online Green Building Course: **www.nachi.org/greenbuildingcoursereleased2007.htm**

- InterNACHI's Green Resources: **www.nachi.org/green**

- Other InterNACHI online courses: **www.nachi.org/education.htm**

- Other InterNACHI online video training courses: **www.nachi.org/advancedcourses.htm**

Appendix I: Answer Keys

Answer Key for Quiz on Section 1

1. T/F: The attached parking structure is not within the scope of a complete mold inspection.
   Answer: **False**

2. T/F: The inspector shall report musty odors.
   Answer: **True**

3. There are two types of mold inspections taught in this guide. One is a Limited Mold Inspection. The other is a **Complete** Mold Inspection.

4. T/F: The visual examination of a building is non-invasive.
   Answer: **True**

5. T/F: At least one air sample is required as part of a Complete Mold Inspection.
   Answer: **False**

6. T/F: All sampling shall be performed according to the IAC2 Mold Sampling Procedures available at **www.IAC2.org**.
   Answer: **True**

Answer Key for Quiz on Section 2

1. T/F: The mold inspection is a home (property) inspection.
   Answer: **False**

2. T/F: The inspector shall carefully inspect the electrical panelboard.
   Answer: **False**

3. T/F: The inspector shall identify mold growth that is not readily visible.
   Answer: **False**

4. T/F: The inspector shall report the life expectancy of the roof covering.
   Answer: **False**

5. T/F: Inspecting for wood-destroying insects is within the scope of a Complete Mold Inspection.
   Answer: **False**

6. T/F: The mold inspector is not required to lift carpeting to detect apparent mold growth.
   Answer: **True**

7. **Apparent mold** is visible growth with characteristics of mold, which cannot be confirmed by the inspector without the benefit of sampling.

Answer Key for Quiz on Section 4

1. T/F: Molds are part of the kingdom Fungi.
   Answer: <u>**True**</u>

2. The main role of fungi in the ecosystem is to <u>**break down dead materials**</u>.

3. T/F: All fungi is mold, but not all mold is fungi.
   Answer: <u>**False**</u>

4. Two common types of indoor mold are *Penicilllium* and *<u>Aspergillus</u>*.

5. People who have concerns about the health effects of mold exposure <u>**should seek the advice of a healthcare professional**</u>.

6. A mold has like long, thread-like strings of cells called <u>**hyphae**</u>.

Answer Key for Quiz for Section 5

1. T/F: Dead or alive, mold can cause allergic reactions in some people.
   Answer: <u>**True**</u>

2. T/F: Children are usually not affected by mold exposure more severely or sooner than other types of people.
   Answer: <u>**False**</u>

3. Current evidence indicates that <u>**allergies**</u> are the types of disease most often associated with molds.

4. T/F: There are four important indoor allergenic molds. They are *Penicillium*, *Aspergillus*, *Cladosporium* and *Alternaria*.
   Answer: <u>**True**</u>

5. As some molds grow under certain conditions, some of them may produce potentially toxic byproducts called <u>**mycotoxins**</u>.

6. T/F: Mold can cause asthma attacks.
   Answer: <u>**True**</u>

Answer Key for Quiz on Section 7

1. A(n) <u>**building**</u> is comprised of an abundant supply of nutrients for mold growth.

2. Once a building is affected by <u>**moisture intrusion**</u>, mold can start growing in very little time.

3. <u>**Building science**</u>, in relation to mold, is the study of the building's dynamics as affected by moisture intrusion.

4. Mold growth can be limited if the MC of wood can be kept below <u>**20%**</u>. Below a <u>**17%**</u> MC of wood, virtually no microbial growth will occur on even the most susceptible materials.

5. T/F: RH is a factor in determining how much moisture is present in a room, but it is the available moisture in a substrate (not the RH of the room's air) that determines if mold can grow or not.
Answer: **True**

6. T/F: To control condensation in a building's exterior walls in cold climates, install air or vapor barriers on the warm side of the building's envelope.
Answer: **True**

7. T/F: Humidifiers should be considered potential sources of mold growth.
Answer: **True**

Answer Key for Quiz on Section 8

1. A(n) **visual** inspection is the most important first step in identifying possible mold contamination.

2. T/F: The inspector shall report moisture intrusion, water damage, musty odors, apparent mold growth, or conditions conducive to mold growth.
Answer: **True**

3. T/F: Inspecting toilets is beyond the scope of a mold inspection.
Answer: **False**

4. Exposed dirt floors in **under-floor crawlspaces** should be sealed with a vapor barrier.

5. T/F: There is no reason to suspect mold if a building has a moldy smell but you don't see any mold.
Answer: **False**

6. T/F: Steam radiators are components whose operation is conducive to mold growth.
Answer: **True**

7. T/F: Excessive watering of house plants may create a condition conducive to mold growth.
Answer: **True**

8. T/F: A lawn sprinkler could create a condition conducive to mold growth.
Answer: **True**

9. T/F: It is possible to perform a professional and thorough mold inspection without a moisture meter.
Answer: **False**

10. T/F: A dryer vent that exhausts into the interior of the building is not within the scope of concern for a mold inspector.
Answer: **False**

11. T/F: An increase (up to 90%) in the relative humidity of air downstream of cooling coils is a natural result of the energy transfer between the air and the coils.
Answer: **True**

12. T/F: Mold needs some light to grow; it cannot grow in areas of complete darkness.
Answer: **False**

13. T/F: Micro-organisms can grow on the damp filter of an HVAC system, and even on the collected dust of its filter.
    Answer: **True**

14. T/F: Poor or delayed maintenance of the HVAC system is a condition conducive to mold growth.
    Answer: **True**

Answer Key for Quiz on Section 10

1. Before taking any samples, an inspector should develop a set of **hypotheses** that address the concerns of the client.

2. "Stains and odors are caused by the presence of mold" is an example of a(n) **aesthetic** hypothesis.

3. T/F: Not everything that looks like mold is mold.
   Answer: **True**

4. T/F: The mold sampling should be in alignment with the client's concerns about mold.
   Answer: **True**

Answer Key for Quiz on Section 17

1. T/F: There have been studies of mold in homes that have provided new information about what is normal or unusual in a healthy home.
   Answer: **True**

2. T/F: In general, the levels and types of fungi found should be significantly different indoors as compared to outdoors.
   Answer: **False**

3. T/F: The information expected from contact surface samples is often just simple confirmation that the collected material is biological in nature, or that biological growth can be ruled out.
   Answer: **True**

4. T/F: Visible, apparent mold, mold-damaged materials, and moldy odors should not be present in a healthy building.
   Answer: **True**

5. T/F: Information on cause-and-effect relationships between biological materials and illness is not currently available.
   Answer: **True**

6. T/F: Samples should be analyzed according to the methods recommended by the American Industrial Hygiene Association (AIHA), the American Conference of Governmental Industrial Hygienists (ACGIH), or other professional guidelines.
   Answer: **True**

7. T/F: It is the mold inspector's responsibility to establish that the client has been exposed to mold spores or that the client's exposure is a health hazard.
   Answer: **False**

Answer Key for Quiz on Section 19

1. T/F: The Scope of Work should list all of the hypotheses (concerns), along with a description of the sampling that was performed in order to test them.
Answer: **True**

2. T/F: The report should include the property's address, size and age of the building, the color of the entry door, number of occupants, and the date of the inspection.
Answer: **False**

3. T/F: The weather conditions should not be included in the report.
Answer: **False**

4. T/F: The sampling devices and sampling locations should be recorded in the report.
Answer: **True**

5. T/F: Interpretation of the results and recommendations should be confined to those that are supported directly by data obtained during the visual examination.
Answer: **True**

Answer Key for Quiz on Section 23

1. Mold can generally be removed from hard surfaces by wiping or scrubbing with **water and detergent**.

2. Mold can grow **instantly** if adequate temperature, moisture and nutrients are provided.

3. T/F: The use of a biocide or a chemical that kills organisms such as mold (chlorine bleach, for example) is recommended as a routine practice during mold cleanup.
Answer: **False**

4. **Containment** should be designed to prevent the movement of mold spores from one area of the building to another.

5. Because exposures may be greatly increased in a confined space, workers must use a higher level of **PPE** than they would when working in a more accessible area.

Answer Key for Quiz on Section 26

1. T/F: The key to mold prevention is moisture control.
Answer: **True**

2. A furnace's **humidifiers** must be cleaned regularly to prevent mold and bacterial growth.

3. T/F: To prevent mold growth, air filters of an HVAC system should be kept dry and changed frequently.
Answer: **True**

4. Vent moisture-generating appliances, such as dryers, to the **outdoors**, where possible.

5. T/F: To prevent mold growth, do not let foundations stay wet.
   Answer: **True**

6. T/F: A remediation clearance inspection is simply a Compete Mold Inspection performed in accordance with the IAC2 Mold Inspection Standards of Practice following remediation.
   Answer: **True**

Notes

EDUCATION & TRAINING BOOKS

Whether you're new to the business, an inspector seeking more information, or a veteran of the industry looking to expand your knowledge, these official InterNACHI publications will help you become the best inspector you can be.

We Offer the Following Education & Training Books:

- **How to Inspect the Exterior**
  Item Number: 0094

- **How to Perform Deck Inspections**
  Item Number: 0029

- **Residential Plumbing Overview**
  Item Number: 0064

- **Inspecting HVAC Systems**
  Item Number: 0061

- **Safe Practices for the Home Inspector**
  Item Number: 0038

- **Inspecting the Attic, Insulation, Ventilation & Interior**
  Item Number: 0109

- **How to Perform Electrical Inspections**
  Item Number: 0023

- **How to Inspect Pools & Spas**
  Item Number: 0076

- **How to Perform Roof Inspections**
  Item Number: 0042

- **How to Perform a Mold Inspection**
  Item Number: 0022

- **How to Perform Radon Inspections**
  Item Number: 0028

- **Inspecting Foundation Walls and Piers**
  Item Number: 0065

- **25 Standards Every Inspector Should Know**
  Item Number: 0037

- **How to Inspect for Moisture Intrusion**
  Item Number: 0073

- **International Standards of Practice for Inspecting Commercial Properties**
  Item Number: 0016

- **Structural Issues for Home Inspectors**
  Item Number: 0059

The purpose of these publications is to provide accurate and useful information for home inspectors in order to perform an inspection of the various systems at a residential property. They also serve as study aids for InterNACHI's online courses, as well as reference manuals for on the job.

Find these books plus more tools to grow your inspection business at
www.InspectorOutlet.com